NATIONAL
GEOGRAPHIC
KiDS

IT'S A NUMBERS GAME! BASEBALL

The math behind the perfect pitch, the game-winning grand slam, and so much more!

James Buckley, Jr.

Foreword by MLB Superstar SEAN DOOLITTLE

NATIONAL GEOGRAPHIC
WASHINGTON, D.C.

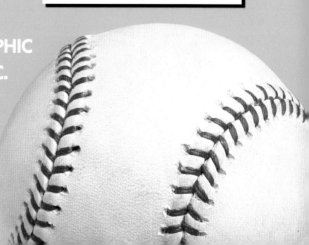

TABLE OF CONTENTS

The statistical data in this book are through 2019 seasons, unless otherwise noted.

It was the bottom of the eighth inning during game 1 of the 2019 World Series. My team, the Washington Nationals, was winning, but not by much. The score was 5–3 in our favor. I heard a phone ring in the bullpen. My bullpen coach picked it up, listened for a moment, hung up the phone, and pointed to me. "Doo, you'll go in to pitch if the Astros get to the third hitter in their lineup."

I had never pitched in a World Series game before. I looked up at the scoreboard to see which hitter was about to step up to the plate. It was their ninth hitter, which meant that the next was their first hitter. I quickly calculated how many warm-up pitches I could throw in the bullpen during the next two hitters before I came into the game. "Eight or nine pitches maybe?" I needed to throw enough warm-up pitches to feel comfortable with my delivery, but I didn't want to throw too many so that I tired myself out before I ever stepped on the mound!

I quickly fired off eight warm-up pitches. I like even numbers. Then I looked at the scouting report on the Astros' third hitter. He was a left-handed hitter. He had hit 19 home runs against right-handed pitchers that season. But he had only hit three home runs against left-handed pitchers that season. I counted my blessings that I'm a left-handed pitcher. As we say in baseball, we were going to play the percentages.

Meanwhile in the game, the Astros' first hitter lined a double into center field, scoring one run. The score was now 5–4, but there were two outs. I dug a little deeper. "Okay..." I thought, "the Astros have the tying run on second base right now, and their third hitter has an on-base percentage (OBP) of .466 when his team has a runner on second base!" That meant he was able to get on base 46.6 percent of the time in that situation. That's almost half the time! I was going to have to buckle down to make sure this would be one of the 53.4 percent of his at bats when he didn't reach base. I threw two more warm-up pitches for good luck.

The phone rang again. My bullpen coach picked up the phone, pointed to me, and said, "Doo, you're in." I took four deep breaths before taking the first step out of the bullpen and on to the biggest stage I'd ever pitched on. It seemed like all of the 43,339 fans at Minute Maid Park were on their feet. The stadium speakers boomed, "Now coming in to pitch: number 63, Sean Doolittle!"

That's a lot of numbers, right? But it's not just the World Series that's packed with digits. Whether you play at the professional, college, or Little League level, numbers track just about everything you do on the field. From the distance you have to throw the ball from the mound to home plate, to the number of balls and strikes, to all the players' statistics, they're a huge part of the game.

Statistics, the score, and the inning might be some obvious numbers in baseball, but there are even more digits in places where you'd least expect it. A batter is faced with numbers when I throw a 95-mile-an-hour (153 km/h) fastball. He has 250 milliseconds to decide if he's going to take a swing at it. My best pitch is my four-seam fastball. If I throw it right, I can make the ball spin with 2,300 rotations per minute (RPM) at 96 miles an hour (155 km/h) in the 60 feet 6 inches (18.4 m) between the pitcher's mound and home plate.

Whether you're hitting dingers on your school's team, keeping track of numbers in a scorebook while you watch your favorite team on TV, or just a math fanatic, you're bound to pick up some helpful tips in *It's a Numbers Game! Baseball*. This book is your guide to all the digits and calculations of baseball so you'll have a better understanding of the sport. Check out baseball's fascinating history and read about the game's heroes and their amazing statistics. I love learning about Randy Johnson's incredible pitching statistics. He had the most strikeouts of any left-handed pitcher in the history of Major League Baseball with 4,875! Each chapter ends with fun games and activities you can do with your friends and family.

So whether you're a first baseman, outfielder, or pitcher like me, or if you just love the game, get ready to slide into some serious digits. Because what is baseball without numbers? Play ball!

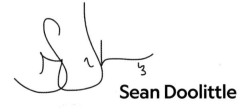

Sean Doolittle

SEAN DOOLITTLE WINDS UP FOR A PITCH IN THE 2019 WORLD SERIES.

CHAPTER ONE

THE FIELD.

THE *GEAR,* AND MORE

L et's get started on our stat-packed trip through the world of baseball. We'll head out to the diamond, run around the bases, and walk the outfield as we look at the basics of the game. Where is it played? How is the field set up? What's the deal with those bats, balls, and gloves? Put on your batting helmet, because it's time to step up to the plate.

FROM PICKUP GAMES TO THE PROS

Major League Baseball (MLB) is the highest level of play in the sport. Today, 30 teams are part of MLB, which is made up of the American League (AL) and the National League (NL). Way back in the late 1800s, the NL began play, followed by the AL in 1901. Since then, they have combined to make MLB. Even though they are under one umbrella organization, they operate as separate leagues with their own standings. At the end of each season, the AL and NL champs face off in the World Series.

THE DIAMOND

Most of baseball's action is on the dazzling diamond. We're not talking a shiny gem, but the shape of the field. This diamond has perfect dimensions. The precise distances on the field make the game play thrilling. For example, because of the placement of first base, just about every play there comes close to being either safe or out. The dimensions of the diamond make it fair for both the players on defense and for the hitters.

ONE BASE TO ANOTHER

So how did the basepath, the lane from one base to the next, get to be exactly 90 feet (27.4 m)? It started with "paces." In baseball's early days, around the mid-1800s, each team used a slightly different field. The general rule to setting up a field was to step "30 paces" before you set down one of the bases. Generally speaking, a pace is about a yard, or three feet (0.9 m) long. But some people have longer legs—and therefore longer strides—than others, which means basepath lengths differed from field to field. In 1857, a large group of baseball clubs got together to agree on how to play the game. They wrote a document that spelled out the official rules. This document is the first written evidence of "90 feet" between bases.

19TH-CENTURY ILLUSTRATION

DIGIT-YOU-KNOW?

In 2016, a handwritten version of the 1857 rules was sold at an auction for $3.26 million!

ON THE MOUND

On MLB fields, the distance from the pitcher's mound to home plate is 60 feet 6 inches (18.44 m). Why not just 60 feet (18.29 m)? In baseball's early days, before the 1890s, the distance was actually 45 feet (13.72 m), but that space slowly grew until 1893, when everyone agreed to stop moving it and the current distance was set. The front of the pitching rubber, where the pitcher starts from, is at the center of imaginary lines that connect second and home and first and third. The distance from the back of home plate to the front of the rubber? Sixty feet six inches (18.44 m).

PENCIL POWER

Get ready to test your math chops—how far does a player run after hitting a home run?

ANSWER: 360 feet (109.73 m)—90 feet (27.43 m) for each of the four basepaths

90 ft
(27.43 m)

PITCHER'S MOUND

60 ft 6 in
(18.44 m)

MAKING IT HOME

Why is home plate shaped like a pentagon? The "home" base used to be round, like a dinner plate. In 1899, baseball switched to a square that was set at an angle, like a diamond. The next year, National League officials agreed to "fill in" the top of the square to form a pentagon pointed toward the umpire and catcher. With this configuration, umpires could better see how well the ball lined up with the strike zone. Since then, home plate has been exactly 17 inches (43.18 cm) across.

HOME PLATE

BATTER'S BOX

BATTER'S BOX

CATCHER'S BOX

THE *BALLPARKS*

Did you know that baseball fields come in slightly different shapes? The basepaths and diamonds are the same size at every park. But the shape of the outfield, as defined by the fences at the back, can vary among fields. Older ballparks used to follow the paths of the city streets that ran around them. Newer parks are designed with odd shapes as a tribute to those older designs. Some walls along the outfield curve or jut or angle to make the look more interesting. Regardless of shape, each ballpark is a "field of dreams" for its fans.

STAT STORY

For some fans, one of the best parts about going to a game is the food. The classic ballpark grub is the hot dog, of course. But in some stadiums, you can find everything from lobster rolls to sushi to barbecue. At Globe Life Park in Arlington, Texas, home of the Texas Rangers, you can dig into a two-pound (0.9-kg) chicken tender. Or at Target Field in Minnesota, try to take on the Boomstick, a hot dog that is almost as long as a baseball bat. At other parks, they offer food from around the world like bulgogi, pierogi, and bahn mi.

BAHN MI

- MLB fans eat more than 18 million hot dogs each season.
- Dodgers fans chomp 2.6 million "Dodger Dogs" each season.
- One company that supplies peanuts to stadiums sold more than 3.7 million bags in a single year.
- The average price of a ballpark hot dog is $4.95.

HISTORY BY THE NUMBERS

The oldest ballpark in MLB is Boston's Fenway Park. It was built in 1912. The most famous part of Fenway is the Green Monster. This 37-foot (11.3-m)-tall wall in left field got its name thanks to its huge size and the green paint that was added in 1947. In 2003, the Red Sox added 269 seats atop the wall for a "monster's-eye" view of the action!

These Major League Baseball ballparks have room for the most fans.

BALLPARK (TEAM)	NUMBER OF SEATS
Dodger Stadium (Los Angeles Dodgers)	56,000
Rogers Centre (Toronto Blue Jays)	49,282
Chase Field (Arizona Diamondbacks)	48,686
Globe Life Park (Texas Rangers)	48,114
Safeco Field (Seattle Mariners)	47,715

TONY KEMP OF THE HOUSTON ASTROS MAKES A LEAPING CATCH AT MINUTE MAID PARK.

DIGIT-YOU-KNOW?

Most fields have numbers displayed on the walls of the outfield. These numbers show the distance in feet from home plate to that point on the wall. At ballparks built after 1958, center field fences must be at least 400 feet (122 m) from home plate. Older parks were allowed to keep their "short" fences. The shallowest outfield fence is in Fenway Park. The left field corner is only 310 feet (94.5 m) from home plate. The deepest outfield fence is in center field at Minute Maid Park in Houston, Texas. Gotta whack a homer 409 feet (124.6 m) to clear that.

CAPS, BATS, AND BALLS

Anyone on a playground at recess knows: All you need to play baseball is a ball and a stick. But by the time you turn pro, the bats get bigger, the balls are handmade, and specialized gear is used for all aspects of the game.

CAPS FOR SALE

Baseball made caps cool! Players have been wearing billed caps since the early days of the game. By the mid-1900s, ballplayers found that by making the brim of their old-fashioned caps a bit longer, it helped block the sun from their eyes. The hat was redesigned with a three-inch (7.6-cm) brim to look like the classic cap you see today. Baseball was the first sport to have players wear this new type of cap during the game. Today you can see caps worn on golfers, NFL quarterbacks on the sidelines, and race car drivers after a race. In fact, you can't walk down most streets in the United States without seeing someone in a baseball-style cap.

THE BATS

On the playground, any old bat might do. But in the major leagues, details are everything. Baseball bats at the pro level are made of wood, usually maple, ash, or hickory. MLB rules say that bats cannot be more than 2.61 inches (6.6 cm) in diameter at their thickest part. The length is limited to 42 inches (107 cm). Bats in MLB have to weigh at least 32 ounces (907 g); most are 34 to 35 ounces (964 to 992 g).

STITCH THIS

The company that makes the official MLB caps says that the Miami Marlins logo takes 11,630 stitches to make. That's the most! Compare that to the simple Pittsburgh Pirates logo, a snap at 1,876 stitches!

CORK-AND-RUBBER CENTER

YARN

HAVING A BALL

An MLB ball is made up of two figure-8-shaped pieces of white leather, held together by 108 stitches, and with yards of yarn wound around a cork-and-rubber center.

WEIGHT: 5 to 5.25 ounces (142 to 149 g)

CIRCUMFERENCE: 9 to 9.25 inches (22.9 to 23.5 cm)

SIZE OF CORK/RUBBER CORE: diameter of 13/16 inch (2.06 cm)

AVERAGE NUMBER OF BASEBALLS USED PER MLB GAME: About 13 dozen

DIGIT-YOU-KNOW?

In 2005, MLB estimated it went through 900,000 game balls. In 2019, the number was up to 1,140,000—and that doesn't even include the playoffs!

BATTING HELMETS

Since 1971, MLB batters have been required to wear a hard, plastic batting helmet when they hit. All levels of baseball follow this rule. Many youth leagues call for a metal or hard-plastic cage mask, too. Pitchers don't intend to hit batters, but it can happen and helmets are there to protect your noggin. Safety first.

WEAR IT

The most visible numbers on the field are on the back of each player's jersey. Some teams have the numbers on the front, too. Numbers are assigned randomly to most players, but stars and veterans are often able to choose their own.

It's not just the players who wear numbers. In MLB, umpires wear small numbers that identify them. Additionally, baseball managers as well as the coaches on first and third bases wear full team uniforms with numbers. On some teams, even the batboys get numbers!

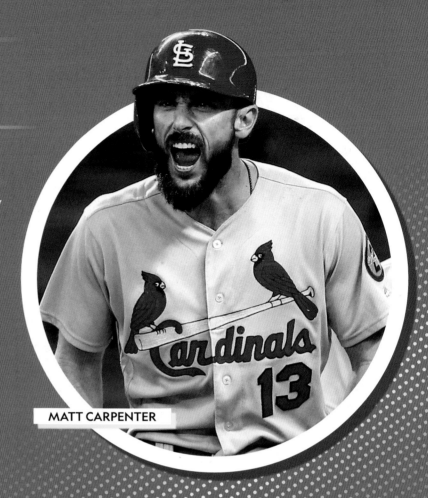

MATT CARPENTER

BABE RUTH

HISTORY BY THE NUMBERS

If you showed up at a big-league baseball game in 1910, you'd notice something very different. Uniforms did not have numbers. MLB teams did not wear numbers until 1929. Some teams tried it a few times before that, but it never caught on. That is until the mighty New York Yankees started the trend. The Yanks wanted to make sure fans could more easily identify their big stars on the field, like Babe Ruth, Lou Gehrig, and Bill Dickey. After that, everyone followed suit. Babe Ruth, the great home run king, was given No. 3 because he batted third. That's how they chose numbers in the early days.

DIGIT-YOU-KNOW?

Carlton Fisk was an All-Star catcher for the Boston Red Sox. He wore 27 with that team. After he moved to the White Sox in 1980, he flipped the digits. His new number? 72!

STAT STORY

- A few ballplayers proudly put 0 on their backs. Can you guess why Al Oliver, Oddibe McDowell, and Adam Ottavino wore their zeroes? (Hint: Check out that round letter that's in all their names.)

- The highest number available is 99. Only a few players have chosen that, including one of the best modern sluggers, the Yankees' Aaron Judge. He was assigned the number during preseason spring training camp. Even when he made the majors and could get a smaller number, he stuck with it.

- As of 2019, the following numbers have never been used by an MLB player: 86, 89, and 92.

ADAM OTTAVINO

HOW DOES A **NUMBER RETIRE?**

In baseball, if a player has a tremendous career and is a longtime fan favorite, he can receive a special honor: His team retires his number. From then on, no other players for that team will wear it. This was done for the first time in 1939 for the great Yankees slugger Lou Gehrig, when he announced he had to retire because he was ill. Read on for more amazing feats and firsts of the athletes behind these retired digits.

 **42**

On April 15, 1947, Jackie Robinson stepped on the field to play first base for the Brooklyn Dodgers. He was the first African American to play in the majors. His courage in helping end the racist ban on Black players, along with his Hall of Fame skill as a player, made him a legend. On April 15, 1997, 50 years after his first game, Major League Baseball retired Robinson's No. 42 for every team in the league.

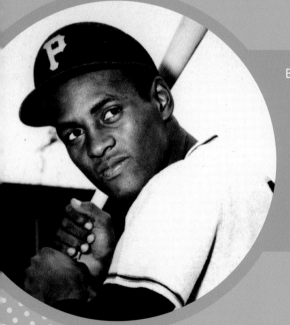

Beginning his MLB career in 1955, Pittsburgh Pirates Hall of Fame outfielder Roberto Clemente was the first baseball star from Puerto Rico and one of the first Hispanic players to become really famous in the United States. Clemente picked the number 21 after counting the letters in his full name: Roberto Clemente Walker. He was as famous for helping others as for his throwing arm and great batting skills. After he died in 1972 in a plane crash—while on his way to deliver relief supplies to earthquake victims—his number was retired by his team.

 **21**

 **26**

After purchasing the team in 1961, cowboy singing star Gene Autry was the owner of the California (now Los Angeles) Angels for 36 years. In 1982, the team retired No. 26 as a way to thank their "26th man" on the 25-man team roster.

44

"Hammerin' Hank" Aaron was the first player to top Babe Ruth's magic career home run total of 714. As an African American who started playing during the 1950s, Aaron was often the target of racist insults and threats. His strength, grace, and perseverance in spite of those obstacles inspired many. His No. 44 was retired by his two teams, the Atlanta Braves and Milwaukee Brewers. Another legendary slugger, Reggie Jackson, who chose 44 in honor of Aaron, also had 44 retired by his team, the New York Yankees.

20

Twenty is the most retired number, with nine players having earned the honor.

LUIS GONZALEZ, Arizona Diamondbacks

FRANK ROBINSON, Baltimore Orioles, Cleveland Indians, Cincinnati Reds

FRANK WHITE, Kansas City Royals

DON SUTTON, Los Angeles Dodgers

JORGE POSADA, New York Yankees

MIKE SCHMIDT, Philadelphia Phillies

PIE TRAYNOR, Pittsburgh Pirates

MONTE IRVIN, San Francisco Giants

LOU BROCK, St. Louis Cardinals

FRANK WHITE

DIGIT-YOU-KNOW?

The New York Yankees have retired the most uniform numbers: 21. Don't look for any more Yankees wearing these digits: 1, 2, 3, 4, 5, 6, 7, 8, 9, 10, 15, 16, 20, 23, 32, 37, 42, 44, 46, 49, 51

SOFTBALL BY THE NUMBERS

S oftball is very much like baseball. So, what are the differences between the two? For one, softballs are larger than baseballs—their minimum circumference is 11 7/8 inches (30.16 cm) around instead of a baseball's minimum of nine inches (22.9 cm). The field also has shorter basepaths, and pitchers are closer to home plate. But the biggest difference is that the pitching is underhand, not overhand. Both slow pitch and fast pitch softball are played.

In truth, baseball and softball share a lot of the same things: Both have nine players on the field, three strikes are an out, and three outs end a half-inning. When it comes to stats, baseball and softball teams record similar ones, such as batting averages and home runs.

SOFTBALL

BASEBALL

OVERHAND THROW

UNDERHAND THROW

THE FIELD

Softball bases are closer together than those in baseball, and on most fields the whole infield is made of dirt, not dirt and grass. Outfield fences are 190 to 220 feet (58 to 67 m) from home plate, depending on the ballpark. Pitchers stand 43 feet (13.1 m) from home plate.

60 ft (18.29 m)

43 ft (13.1 m)

PITCHER'S CIRCLE

HOME PLATE

UCLA STAR RACHEL GARCIA THROWS USING A FAST PITCH MOTION.

STAT STORY

NUMBER OF COLLEGE TEAMS: 1,680

NUMBER OF COLLEGE PLAYERS: 31,000+

NUMBER OF HIGH SCHOOL PLAYERS: 374,000+

LITTLE LEAGUE SOFTBALL: 300,000 players

SOFTBALL STARTS UP

Softball started in the 1890s as a way to play baseball indoors. In the early 1900s, it evolved into an outdoor game. It became popular among female athletes because women were pretty much shut out of playing baseball—none of the guys let them play. The All-American Girls Professional Softball League started in 1943, but it quickly switched its name and game to baseball in 1945 before breaking up in 1954. By the 1960s, women at colleges and on a few pro teams were playing fast pitch softball. Women's softball has been played at the Summer Olympics, and the U.S. teams won three gold medals. Today softballers in the United States play at the professional level in the National Pro Fastpitch (NPF).

MACAULEY PRICKETT OF NC STATE IN 2007

DIGIT-YOU-KNOW?

Monica Abbott was one of the best college softball pitchers ever. In four years at Tennessee ending in 2007, she set career records for games started (206), wins (189), and strikeouts (2,440). She is also second all-time with 23 no-hitters! Continuing to break records in her professional career, in 2016, Abbott became the first woman to sign a million-dollar pro softball contract.

TRY *THIS!*

How to Pick the Right Bat

To be a ballplayer, you gotta pick a solid stick! Here are some ways you can select the right bat. While it's helpful to review all the information and recommendations provided here and by retailers, the most important thing to consider is this: You should choose the bat that feels the best to you.

WHAT YOU NEED:

- A few bats
- A tape measure
- A scale for weighing yourself
- A pencil and paper
- A friend
- Space big enough to swing a bat (outside is best)

WOOD

ALUMINUM

Materials

Just about every youth league uses non-wooden bats. Check with your league to find out what bats are approved. Many use bats that are made of aluminum or a plastic composite.

1 Measuring

Find a good length for your bat by measuring the distance from the middle of your chest to the end of your arm. A good bat length for most young players should be about this length.

Determine the right weight for your bat by picking one up. Can you hold it straight out from your side—with your arm at shoulder height—for 30 to 40 seconds? If you can, that's a good weight. If you can't, it's probably too heavy. Try another bat until you find the best fit.

PROPER LENGTH

40
30

HOLD BAT 30–40 SECONDS

Feel

This is tricky to explain, but the idea is that the bat should feel just right for you. What does that mean? For one, it should not be difficult for you to swing. If you can't swing it easily and smoothly, you'll never hit the ball. However, if your bat is too easy to swing, it might not be heavy enough. That means you're giving up some of the power that comes from the weight of the bat. Practice and trying different weights will help you find the bat that feels just right for you.

Grab a parent and head online. Check out bat seller websites. Several companies provide measurement grids for their bats. Measure your height and find out how much you weigh. You'll need to plug these figures into the provided charts to find out which bat length and weight is recommended for you.

WEIGHT DROP

Bats can be measured by their weight drop, a number that is sometimes included with a bat's sales materials. Weight drop allows you find out how heavy a bat "feels," as opposed to what it actually weighs. If you put more weight at the long end of something, it feels heavier than it would if the weight was evenly distributed.

Let's do the math:

$$\frac{\text{Bat length in inches}}{\text{Bat weight in ounces}} \cdots \text{Weight drop}$$

Example:

$$\frac{34 \text{ inches}}{31 \text{ ounces}} \cdots \text{weight drop of 3}$$

When you find the bat that feels right to you, figure out its weight drop. Then as you improve as a player, you can look for bats with lower weight drop numbers. The lower you can make the weight drop number, the more power you can generate with the bat through your swing. Older and more experienced players tend to use bats with lower drop numbers.

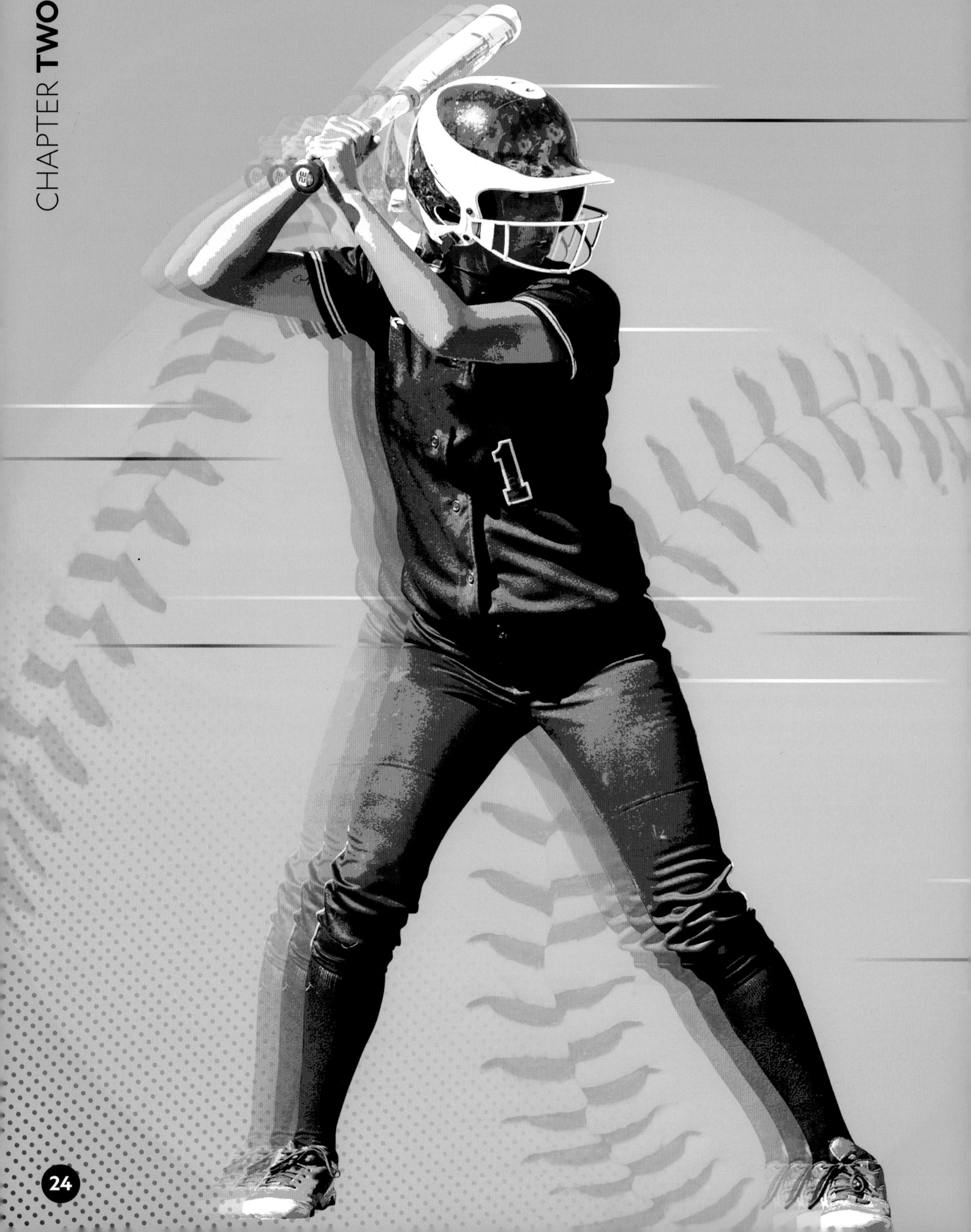
1

CHAPTER TWO

HITTING

A spherical baseball can move toward the bat at more than 90 miles an hour (145 km/h). A tube-like, wooden bat moves toward the ball at about 80 miles an hour (129 km/h). There's an approximately two-inch (5-cm)-long "sweet spot" on a bat—the area that will most likely result in a solidly hit ball. When these three things come together, you have a good chance of having a hit on your hands.

Turns out there are lots of numbers and physics behind hitting a baseball. All of them add up to one truth: Hitting the ball is really difficult! In this chapter, we'll go over all the numbers that fans and players look at to figure out how hitters add up.

THE SWEET SPOT

Want to find a wooden bat's sweet spot? Grab an adult and tell them to bring a hammer. You'll need a wooden bat, too, of course. Hold the bat loosely between your thumb and index finger. Don't squeeze it with the rest of your hand. With the heavy end of the bat hanging down, have the adult start to tap the bat lightly with the hammer. Be careful and be sure to keep your fingers far from the hammer. Feel those vibrations? As the grown-up keeps tapping up the bat, the hammer will hit a point that doesn't make you feel vibrations. Bingo—that's the sweet spot!

COUNT 'EM UP

MITCH HANIGER OF THE SEATTLE MARINERS

Every time a player steps to the plate, the counting begins. Here are some of the ways that hits are counted.

YOU'VE HIT THE BALL: NOW WHAT HAPPENS?

Just connecting the bat with the ball does not mean you got an official hit. Batters are credited with an actual hit only once they reach base, and neither of the following things also happens:

• *FIELDER'S CHOICE:* The batter reaches base, but an out is recorded on another base.

• *ERROR:* A player reaches base, but did so only because the defense made a mistake.

TOTAL BASES (TB)

If you count each base a player reaches from a hit and add them up, that gives you the stat called total bases (TB). A single counts as one base, a double is two, a triple is three, and a homer is four.

A high TB number is awesome; it means you're a great hitter. As you can see, it's much better to hit a lot of doubles, triples, and homers than the same number of singles.

Here's the formula:

(Singles x 1) + (Doubles x 2) + (Triples x 3) + (Home runs x 4) = TB.

So, for example, a batter who has 100 hits made up of 40 singles, 30 doubles, 20 triples, and 10 home runs has collected 200 TB.

So that's

$(40 \times 1) + (30 \times 2) + (20 \times 3) + (10 \times 4) = 40 + 60 + 60 + 40 = 200$ TB.

Singles	Doubles	Triples	Home Runs		
40	30	20	10		40
× 1	× 2	× 3	× 4		60
40	60	60	40		60
					+ 40
					200 TB

If all his 100 hits were singles, his TB would only be 100. By doing the math, you can see that TB gives us a more complete look at how a player records hits.

HITS (H)

Count up all the singles, doubles, triples, and home runs a player gets (counting by ones, that is), and you have a player's total hits.

CAREER RECORD:
PETE ROSE
(1963–86) **4,256**

SINGLES (1B)

Congratulations, batter! You got a hit and made it to first base.

CAREER RECORD:
PETE ROSE
(1963–86) **3,215**

DOUBLES (2B)

This is the first of the hits called "extra-base" hits. It gets the player to second base.

CAREER RECORD:
TRIS SPEAKER
(1907–28) **792**

TRIPLES (3B)

A long hit, a speedy runner, and a cloud of dust. Safe at third with an exciting triple!

CAREER RECORD:
"WAHOO" SAM CRAWFORD
(1899–1917) **309**

HOME RUNS (HR)

Everybody loves the long ball. You hit the ball and make it around all the bases, running to home.

CAREER RECORD:
BARRY BONDS
(1986–2007) **762**

STRIKE ZONE

Any pitch that travels through the imaginary box shown here is called a strike by the umpire. The "strike zone" covers the space above home plate between a batter's chest and below the kneecap.

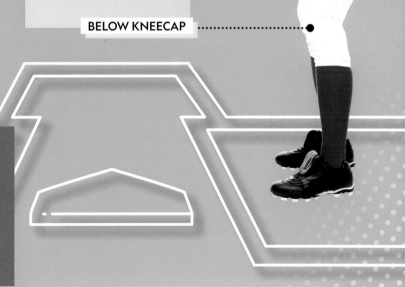

TOP OF SHOULDERS

The midpoint between the top of the shoulders and the top of the pants determines the top of the strike zone.

TOP OF PANTS

STRIKE ZONE

BELOW KNEECAP

WALKS

The best way to get on base without getting a hit is through a walk, also called a base on balls. If the pitcher throws four pitches that the umpire says are outside the strike zone, then the batter gets to go to first base, meaning he gets a walk.

FAMOUS **AVERAGES**

For most of baseball's history, batting average has been the number one way to rank hitters. Average is still very important today, but these days we also consider other stats when evaluating the skills and success of a hitter.

The idea of a batting average was created by a writer named Henry Chadwick in 1867. He wanted a way to compare the success of batters in getting hits. So what does average mean? It's a way to look at approximately how often something happens. A batting average of .300 means that you got three hits out of every 10 at bats. (Keep in mind .300 is the same as 300 out of 1,000 which is the same as 3 out of 10.) If you got three right answers out of 10 on a quiz, that's not considered very good. But three hits out of 10 tries in baseball is really, really good!

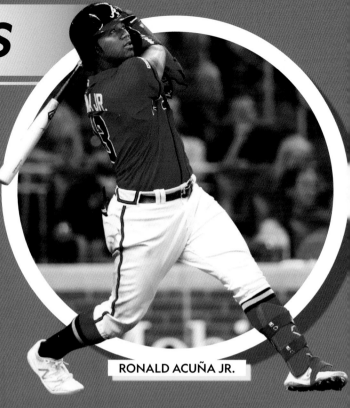

RONALD ACUÑA JR.

DIGIT-YOU-KNOW?

You can calculate batting average (BA) by dividing a player's hits (H) by the number of at bats (AB), or times he or she comes up to hit. An AB means an official at bat, which is whenever you come to the plate minus any walks, sacrifices, and hit by pitches.

Here's the formula: $\dfrac{H}{AB} = BA$

The Atlanta Braves' young star Ronald Acuña, Jr., had 127 hits and 433 ABs in his rookie year. 127 H/ 433 AB = .293

$$\frac{127}{433} = .293$$

TIP
BA is always written without the initial zero and as three digits after a decimal point, such as .293.

THE BEST!

Before 1901, the best average ever was Hugh Duffy's .440 in 1894. Since 1901, when MLB began its "modern" era, the best batting average ever for a single season is Nap Lajoie's, who hit .426 in that same year. The best career batting average belongs to the great Ty Cobb, who batted .367 over 24 seasons. In the 21st century, the highest single-season average is .372. Amazingly, that average was achieved by two players in the same season, 2000—Nomar Garciaparra and Todd Helton. Then Ichiro Suzuki matched them in 2004.

TY COBB

DIGIT-YOU-KNOW?

Only in baseball can you fail seven out of ten times and still be considered a success. As you know, a batting average of .300 is very good. But see how .300 would compare in other sports. These are league-wide averages of plays in each sport from a recent season. They're all better than a .300 hitter. Why does this matter? It shows how hard it is to hit a baseball!

NBA FREE-THROW PERCENTAGE: .766

NHL SAVE PERCENTAGE: .905

NFL FIELD-GOAL PERCENTAGE: .847

BATTER *UP* (OR DOWN)

This chart shows the MLB-wide batting average at various points since 1910. What has happened to BA over time?

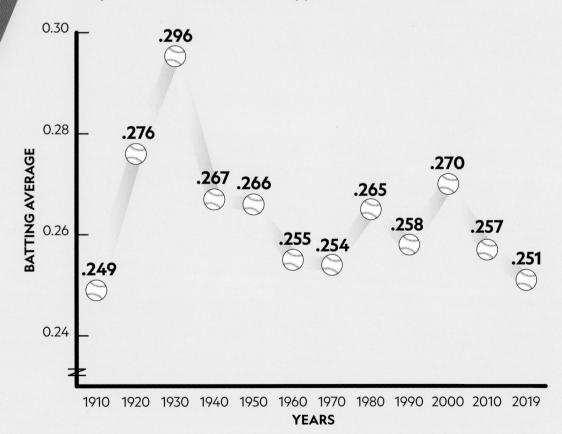

BATTING AVERAGE

.296
.276
.267 .266
.265
.270
.258
.257
.255 .254
.251
.249

YEARS
1910 1920 1930 1940 1950 1960 1970 1980 1990 2000 2010 2019

THE FAQ FOR **OBP** AND **SA**

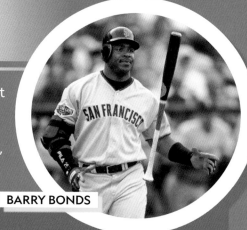
BARRY BONDS

Hits such as singles and doubles are not the only ways batters can get on base. Another stat, called on-base percentage, keeps track of how often batters get on base through hits and various other ways. A third key stat, called slugging average, also called slugging percentage, counts how often a player smacks extra-base hits. Let's calculate!

ON-BASE PERCENTAGE (OBP)

To find this important figure, you need a stack of other stats.

1 Add up all the times a player got on base. This includes the player's hits, walks (also called BB, or bases on balls, the official name for walks), and times he was hit by a pitch (HBP). For BB and HBP, the batter gets to go to first base. That goes on the top of your division problem.

2 Add up walks and hit by pitches again, along with sacrifices (SF, when a batter makes an out on purpose to help a teammate move around the bases). Then add at bats, which are the times the player went up and did not reach base by an error or an HBP or make a sacrifice. That total is on the bottom.

3 Divide the top by the bottom. An OBP of .400 or more is very good because it means the player is getting on base in many other ways besides just hits. In recent seasons, the league-wide average has usually been about .320.

Here's the formula:

$$\frac{H + BB + HBP}{AB + BB + HBP + SF} = OBP$$

In 2019, Mike Trout had 137 hits, 110 walks, 16 hit by pitches, and 4 sacrifices in 470 at bats: 137 H + 110 BB + 16 HBP / 470 AB + 110 BB + 16 HBP + 4 SF = .438 OBP

137 **hits**	470 **at bats**		**.438** OBP
110 **bases on balls (walks)**	110 **bases on balls (walks)**		
+ 16 **hit by a pitch**	16 **hit by a pitch**	$\frac{263}{600}$ →	$600\sqrt{263}$
263	+ 4 **sacrifices**		
	600		

DIGIT-YOU-KNOW?

Seamheads (baseball fans) look at a player's "slash" line. Here they can see most of their favorite hitting data in one place: BA/OBP/SA. For example, 2018 NL MVP Christian Yelich had a slash line that season of .327/.402/.598. As with most averages in baseball, the higher the number the better. Why do we call it a slash line? Check out the punctuation!

SLUGGING AVERAGE

Batting average treats all hits the same. In figuring batting average, a single counts for as many "hits" as a double. But a double is a better hit, right? So how do you compare how many extra-base hits a player gets? That's where slugging average (SA) comes in. Remember total bases from page 26? Slugging average is the number of total bases divided by the number of total official at bats (AB minus walks, errors, and sacrifices).

Here's the formula:

$$\frac{TB}{AB} = SA$$

In 1965, the great Willie Mays had 360 TB in 558 AB. His SA was the best in the majors that season.

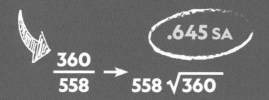

$$\frac{360}{558} \rightarrow 558\sqrt{360} \quad .645\ SA$$

SA RECORD HOLDERS

SINGLE-SEASON RECORD:
BARRY BONDS .**863**
(2001)

CAREER RECORD:
BABE RUTH .**690**
(1914–35)

BABE RUTH

PENCIL POWER

Can you use this chart to figure out Frank Robinson's OBP and SA for these three great seasons? This Hall of Famer was the first player to be named Most Valuable Player (MVP) in both the NL (Reds 1961) and AL (Orioles 1966), and he later served as the first African-American manager. Add up each column for a total number of AB, H, etc. then plug each total into the equations.

FRANK ROBINSON

YEAR	AB	H	HR	RBI	BB	HBP	SF	TB
1960	464	138	31	83	82	9	7	276
1961	545	176	37	124	71	10	10	333
1962	609	208	39	136	76	11	5	380

BONUS: What was his batting average for these seasons?

ANSWER: Totals of SA = .611; OBP = .411; BA = .323

HOME RUNS

The homer. The dinger. The long ball. Jack! Tater! Whatever nickname you use, a homer is the biggest play in the game. In recent seasons, baseballs have been flying out of the yard more than at any time in the game's long history. In 2019, MLB players combined to hit 6,776 homers—a new all-time single-season record! On the next few pages, we'll dive into dingers, mash some taters, and explore where the home run has been and where it's going, going, gone!

KOLTEN WONG #16 AND JOSE MARTINEZ #38 OF THE ST. LOUIS CARDINALS HIGH-FIVE.

SINGLE-SEASON STARS

Before 1998, only two players had ever reached 60 homers in a season: Babe Ruth in 1927 (60 HR) and Roger Maris in 1961 (61 HR). Babe did it in 151 games (the MLB season was only 154 games long then). Maris hit his 61st in his 161st game; MLB had expanded its schedule to 162 games that year. In 1998, Mark McGwire of the St. Louis Cardinals and Sammy Sosa of the Chicago Cubs staged the greatest home run battle ever. Late in the season, McGwire joined Ruth and Maris in the 60-homer club. Sosa reached that magic mark a few games later. By the end of that homer-happy season, McGwire had the new record at 70; Sosa reached 66. Three years later, Barry Bonds of the Pittsburgh Pirates beat them both by smacking 73 homers.

MARK MCGWIRE

SAMMY SOSA

32

CAREER LEADERS

The greatest home run hitter of all time? Depends who you ask. Take a look at this list of players with the most career home runs.

PLAYER	CAREER HOMERS
Barry Bonds	762
Hank Aaron	755
Babe Ruth	714
Alex Rodriguez	696
Willie Mays	660
Albert Pujols*	656
Ken Griffey, Jr.	630
Jim Thome	612
Sammy Sosa	609

(*Active in 2019)

HANK AARON

MIAMI MARLIN GIANCARLO STANTON HITS A HOME RUN AGAINST THE ATLANTA BRAVES IN 2017.

BAD STATS

In the late 20th century into the early 21st, the use of steroids seemed to be on the rise in Major League Baseball. Steroids are chemicals designed to make a person unnaturally strong and powerful. It was a huge scandal that damaged the sport. Some players got caught and were suspended, fined, and even banned from MLB. Additional players were suspected but not caught, so while MLB recognizes all those records as official, the single-season home run record is now questionable in the eyes of many fans and experts.

MORE HOME RUN RECORDS

You like home runs? We got home runs! We've got base-balls flying out of the yard in just about every way you can think of! Check out this dugout full of long ball memories.

MOST GRAND SLAMS

A grand slam is the best homer you can hit. When there is a teammate on every base (also called "bases loaded" or "bases full") and you smack the ball out of the park, you get four runs for your team. Here are the players with the most grand slams ever:

PLAYER	GRAND SLAMS
Alex Rodriguez	25
Lou Gehrig	23
Manny Ramirez	21
Eddie Murray	19
Willie McCovey	18
Robin Ventura	18

ALEX RODRIGUEZ

GAME AFTER GAME

In 2019, the New York Yankees set a new MLB record by cracking at least one homer in 31 straight games! Earlier that season, the Seattle Mariners set a record for the start of a season with 20 in a row from Opening Day onward. (The Los Angeles Dodgers put together a streak of 33 home games, but that included some from late in the 2018 season and some from early in 2019.) What is the longest streak by a player? Dale Long (1956), Don Mattingly (1987), and Ken Griffey, Jr. (1993) each tied for the best with eight straight games hitting a dinger.

JOE CARTER

MOST INSIDE-THE-PARK HOME RUNS

Wait, doesn't the ball have to leave the ballpark to be a home run? Nope. You can hit an inside-the-park homer. It usually takes speed and a lucky bounce or two. Ballparks used to have much larger outfields, so inside-the-parkers are much more rare today. Here are the five players with the most all-time inside-the-park homers.

Jesse Burkett, 55 (1890–1905)

Sam Crawford, 51 (1899–1917)

Tommy Leach, 48 (1898–1918)

Ty Cobb, 46 (1905–28)

Honus Wagner, 46 (1897–1917)

HISTORY BY THE NUMBERS

So many of us have had the dream in which we hit a home run in the bottom of the ninth inning to win the World Series. Turns out, it really is like a fantasy; it has happened only twice in baseball history!

1960: With Game 7 tied at 9–9, the Pittsburgh Pirates' Bill Mazeroski ended the game and the World Series with a homer to left field. The Pirates upset the mighty New York Yankees, and "Maz" became a Pittsburgh hero forever.

1993: It was only Game 6, but Joe Carter ended it and the Series with a huge homer. His Toronto Blue Jays beat the Philadelphia Phillies. No one has ended the Series with a homer since!

PRIMED FOR **LAUNCH**

In recent seasons, MLB started using a new way of tracking and measuring home runs. Cameras track every movement of the ball, and computers quickly calculate information using a system called Statcast. As players and coaches study the Statcast data, they develop new ways to go after the long ball. Of course, players always want to hit it on the sweet spot, which is the point on the bat (about 2–3 inches [5–8 cm] wide) where the most power is transferred from the swing to the ball.

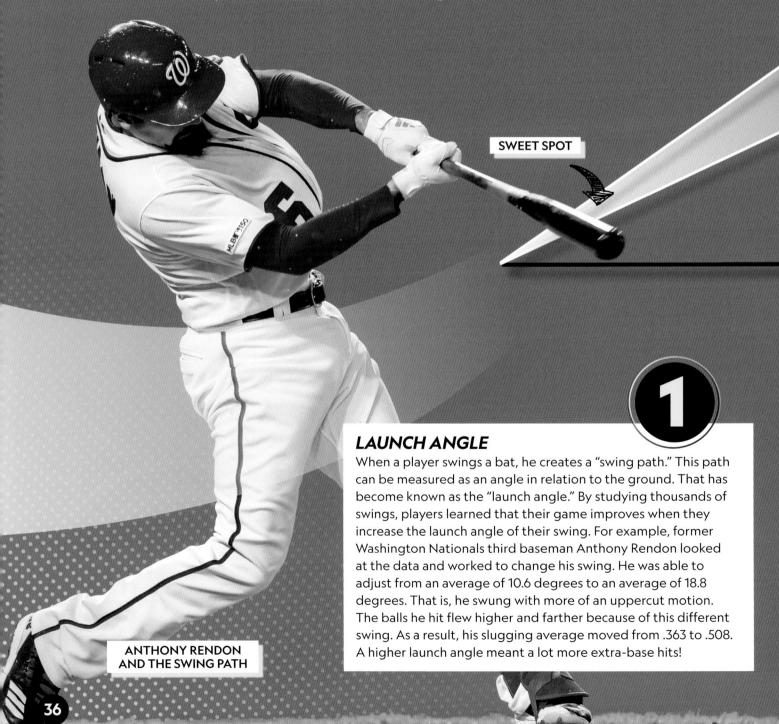

SWEET SPOT

ANTHONY RENDON
AND THE SWING PATH

1

LAUNCH ANGLE

When a player swings a bat, he creates a "swing path." This path can be measured as an angle in relation to the ground. That has become known as the "launch angle." By studying thousands of swings, players learned that their game improves when they increase the launch angle of their swing. For example, former Washington Nationals third baseman Anthony Rendon looked at the data and worked to change his swing. He was able to adjust from an average of 10.6 degrees to an average of 18.8 degrees. That is, he swung with more of an uppercut motion. The balls he hit flew higher and farther because of this different swing. As a result, his slugging average moved from .363 to .508. A higher launch angle meant a lot more extra-base hits!

25-35°

SPEED EQUALS HOMERS

The faster a hitter swings his bat, the more force he can transfer to a ball. Guess how that helps hitters? More force equals more power equals more homers! Statcast calculates bat speed as "exit velocity." That is, how fast the baseball is moving as it leaves the player's bat. The Yankees' Giancarlo Stanton has topped 120 miles an hour (193 km/h) in exit velocity.

0°

UP AND UP AND *UP!*

Here's a chart of the total home runs hit in the major leagues over the past 10 years. Notice anything?

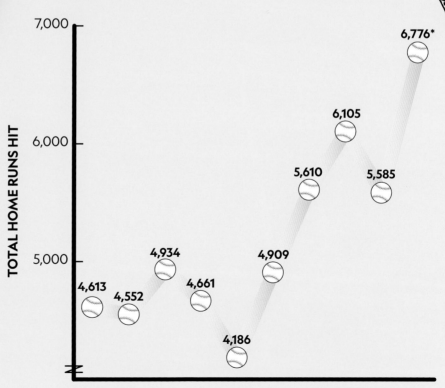

TOTAL HOME RUNS HIT

7,000 — 6,776*

6,105

6,000 — 5,610 · 5,585

5,000 — 4,934 · 4,909 · 4,613 · 4,552 · 4,661 · 4,186

2010 2011 2012 2013 2014 2015 2016 2017 2018 2019

YEARS

* See how the chart shows a progression upward? That means that over time, more home runs have been recorded.

GOING, GOING, *GONE*

Along with data on launch angle and exit speed, MLB can now accurately measure the distance of home runs. Cameras track the launch angle, speed, and direction of the ball. Computers then calculate how far the ball went. Fans *love* this! Until MLB introduced Statcast, teams could only estimate the distance of a homer. Now, within seconds after it leaves the bat, fans can learn exactly how far the ball went.

STATCAST CAMERAS TRACK THE ACTION ON THE FIELD AND LET FANS GET GAME DATA SUPER FAST.

LONG BALLS!

These are the 10 longest home runs hit since Statcast began measuring long balls in 2015.

PLAYER, TEAM, YEAR	DISTANCE (FT/M)
Nomar Mazara, Texas Rangers, 2019	505/154
Trevor Story, Colorado Rockies, 2018	505/154
Giancarlo Stanton, Miami Marlins, 2016	504/153.6
Aaron Judge, New York Yankees, 2017	495/151
Kris Bryant, Chicago Cubs, 2015	495/151
Gary Sánchez, New York Yankees, 2017	493/150.3
Michael Taylor, Washington Nationals, 2015	493/150.3
Nelson Cruz, Seattle Mariners, 2016	493/150.3
Joey Gallo, Texas Rangers, 2017	490/149.3
Franchy Cordero, San Diego Padres, 2018	489/149

DIGIT-YOU-KNOW?

In finishing second in the 2019 Home Run Derby, Vladimir Guerrero, Jr., smashed an incredible 91 homers in his three rounds of hitting. He lost in the final round to Pete Alonso, but "Vladdy" became a legend. Turns out, his 91 dingers traveled a farther distance than anyone could have imagined: a total of 7.3 miles (11.7 km).

HOME RUN DERBY

Fans love homers so much that MLB has a special event each summer called the Home Run Derby in which players do nothing but hit long balls. The whole point is to see who can hit the most homers during a set period of time. It's more like batting practice than a game, since the pitchers throw softer to try to give the hitters something perfect to smack. The rules have varied over the years, but the Derby usually ends up with a head-to-head contest between two finalists.

NOMAR MAZARA

HITTING HEROES

Among the nearly 20,000 people who have played in MLB, who are some of the best at whacking the ol' ball? Everyone has different opinions on who is the best hitter ever, but below are some indisputable champs. Who would you include on your list and why?

HONUS WAGNER

Years Active: 1897–1917

"The Flying Dutchman" did everything well on a baseball field. Big and strong, he was also incredibly fast. Playing for the Pittsburgh Pirates, he led the NL in hitting eight times. He was also top in doubles seven times. His 3,420 hits are eighth all-time.

BABE RUTH

Years Active: 1914–35

There is not enough room here for all the amazing hitting feats of the Bambino. He smacked homers like no one before him and few since, leading the AL in that stat an incredible 12 times. He was so feared that he led the league in walks 11 times, too!

WILLIE MAYS

Years Active: 1951–73

Willie Mays excelled not just at one thing, but at all the important things in this game. He could run like the wind and had a powerful throwing arm. In the outfield, he earned 12 Gold Gloves for fielding excellence. He could hit with power (660 career homers) and for batting average (.302 career). The "Say Hey Kid" was an all-around great.

HANK AARON

Years Active: 1954–76

"Hammerin' Hank" earned his nickname for his home run stroke. He had 40 or more in eight seasons on his way to beating the Babe and reaching 755 for his career. Perhaps more importantly, Aaron helped his team. He is the all-time leader in RBIs (runs batted in, or when another player makes it home because of your hit) with 2,297.

ALBERT PUJOLS

Years Active: 2001–present
Pujols was one of the best players of the first decade of the 2000s. A batting, home run, and RBI champ, he was clutch for the Cardinals. He won three Most Valuable Player awards and finished second in the voting four other times. He moved to the Angels in 2012.

ICHIRO SUZUKI

Years Active: 2001–19
Born in Japan, Suzuki was already a legend in his home country when he jumped to the majors in 2001. He took the sport by storm, winning MVP and Rookie of the Year, along with having the highest AL batting average. Three years later, he broke a record many thought was untouchable when he cracked 262 hits in one season. He became the first ever to top 200 hits in 10 straight seasons. Seemingly able to hit any pitch anywhere, he was a master at the bat.

MIKE TROUT

Years Active: 2011–present
This Angels outfielder is recognized by fans and players alike as one of the best all-around players in the game. He has won two MVP awards and has the highest WAR (see page 82) in the AL in seven of the past eight seasons, and in 2019 he had the highest OPS+ (see page 84) in baseball since 2016. He also led in OBP from 2016–19, and he has led in runs scored four times. How feared is Trout at the plate? In three seasons, he led the league in intentional walks—teams walked him on purpose rather than give him a chance to hit!

TRY *THIS!*

Life Is More Than Just Batting Average

Percentages, or averages, are a big deal in baseball stats. Remember, a percentage basically shows how often something happens. For instance, if a player gets 4 hits in 10 at bats, that's 40 percent, or an average of .400. (And that's really good!). But averages aren't just for baseball! They can be found all over your life, too.

You may know about grade point average, or GPA. Instead of dividing hits and at bats, GPA uses grades and classes to tell how well a student has done. What else can we average?

1 Grab a sheet of paper and create a handful of two-column charts with the activities listed here. In the first column, list an activity, and in the second column, list a change that could make that activity slightly different. Then keep track of these activities over the course of a week.

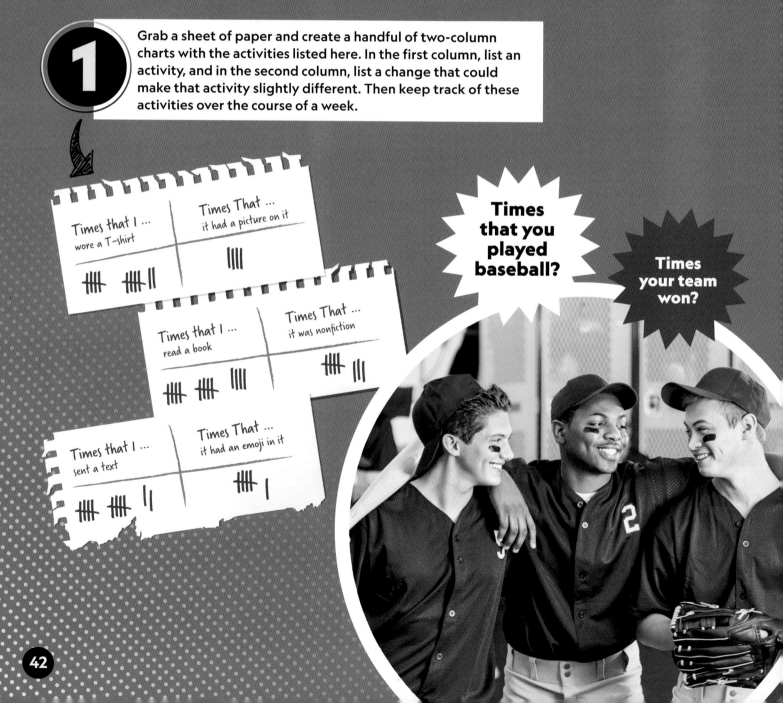

Times that I ... wore a T-shirt	Times That ... it had a picture on it
卌 卌||	||||

Times that I ... read a book	Times That ... it was nonfiction
卌 卌 ||||	卌 |||

Times that I ... sent a text	Times That ... it had an emoji in it
卌 卌 ||	卌	

Times that you played baseball?

Times your team won?

Times that you pet an animal?

Times it was a dog?

Times that you rode a bike?

Times you biked up a hill?

2 When the week is over, tally up the numbers. Figure out what your "batting" average is for each activity using the equation below. How'd you do?

Here's a reminder of the formula, using baseball as an example:

$$\frac{H}{AB} = BA$$ **(hits divided by at bats equals batting average)**

Or, look at it a different way:
Times you ate a meal with fruit divided by the number of meals = your fruit-eating average.

ate a meal	you had fruit with it	Average
20	8	.400

 $$\frac{8}{20} = .400$$

CHAPTER THREE

PITCHING

There's an old baseball saying: Hitting is the art of timing. That is, you have to time your swing just right to connect your bat with a fast-moving ball. Funnily enough, another saying is: Pitching is the art of *ruining* that timing!

Pitchers use different tools to fool hitters. They can throw the ball extremely fast to blow it past the batter, or they can make the ball curve and move in such a way that misleads the hitter. The greatest pitchers do both. That makes the battle between hitter and pitcher a constant guessing game: What will he throw next?

All those pitches add up to lots of stats and numbers, of course, so let's toe the slab (that's slang for standing on the pitching rubber at the center of the mound) and check out some pitchers.

DIGIT-YOU-KNOW?

Left-handed people make up about 10 percent of the world's population. MLB teams hope that a lot of those people turn out to be pitchers. Why? Left-handed batters usually have a tougher time hitting against left-handed pitchers, so having southpaws around is pretty useful. In recent seasons, left-handed pitchers threw about 25 percent of total innings pitched.

WINS, LOSSES, AND SAVES

At the end of every baseball game, one pitcher is the listed as the winner and one as the losing pitcher. The winner is the pitcher who is in the game when his team goes ahead to stay, which means his team takes the lead and at no time after that point does the other team score enough runs to tie or take the lead. This can often be the starting pitcher, if he has gone at least five innings. There are also a bunch of rules that say who ends up "on the hook" for the loss.

WARREN SPAHN

THE BIG WINNERS

Starting pitchers get most of the wins, so the names on these lists are all starters. Before the 1980s or so, starting pitchers threw in many more games and for more innings. In fact, before the creation of the American League in 1901, many teams only used two or three pitchers. In recent years, starters have gotten more help from relief pitchers as team strategies have changed. It's not unheard of for a team to use more than a dozen pitchers in a game. That's why so many records for wins are old.

Most career wins: Cy Young, 511

Most career wins by a lefty: Warren Spahn, 363

Most wins in a season (post-1901): Jack Chesbro, 41 (1904)

Most wins in a row without losing: Carl Hubbell, 24 (1936–37)

CY YOUNG

HISTORY BY THE NUMBERS

Denton True "Cy" Young stands atop the all-time wins list, and he'll probably be there forever. But he's also on top of the all-time losses list! Pitchers today rarely top 20 wins in a season, let alone 30, which Young did five times. He was extraordinarily talented, and in those days pitchers threw a lot more innings and games, so he had more chances to earn wins—and losses. After he played from 1890 to 1911, he was one of the first people elected to the Baseball Hall of Fame in 1937. In 1956, MLB named its annual award for best pitcher after Young.

FRANCISCO RODRIGUEZ

SAVES

The pitcher who comes in to shut down an opponent at the end of the game is called the closer. If that pitcher is successful, he earns a save. A "blown save" means the closer didn't shut the opponent down, and they came back to tie or win the game. Here are some key records for saves.

Most in a career: Mariano Rivera, 652

Most in a season: Francisco Rodriguez, 62 (2008)

LOSSES

A pitcher earns the loss if he starts and then his team falls behind in the score and never comes back. A relief pitcher can earn the loss by giving up runs that put his team behind and unable to come back. In some cases, though, it's not the pitcher's fault. His team members might be making errors or not scoring very many runs.

*Note: All single-season records on these pages are from the 1901 season onward; that's when the AL was born, creating the two major leagues. It's known as baseball's "modern era."

MARIANO RIVERA

STRIKE THREE, BALL FOUR, AND MORE

Every time a batter faces a pitcher, there is an outcome. That is, either the pitcher gets the batter out or the batter somehow reaches a base. Pitchers rack up several key stats during these encounters that add up over a season and a career. Pitchers can strike a batter out by getting three strikes. These are either called by the umpire when the ball goes through the strike zone, or the ball is swung at and missed by the batter. The first two foul balls in an at bat are also strikes. Pitchers can walk a batter by throwing four pitches outside the strike zone for "balls." If they hit a batter with the pitch, he gets to go to first base; that's a "hit by pitch" (HBP). Ouch! And, of course, pitchers can give up base hits, which they hate to do. Let's look at the good, the bad, and the really, really good.

THE K ZONE

The strikeout is the most famous of all the pitching stats. Putting up a lot of Ks, which is shorthand for strikeouts, is a sure sign of a pitcher's dominance. With each recent year of play, Ks have become even more common. There are a lot of reasons for this, but two main ones are that pitchers are throwing faster than ever and hitters are generally trying to hit homers, thus swinging in such a way that they miss more pitches. The number of strikeouts in baseball rose for 13 seasons in a row through 2019.

Most career strikeouts: Nolan Ryan, 5,714

Most strikeouts in a season: Nolan Ryan, 383 (1973)

DIGIT-YOU-KNOW?

Pitchers who plunk the most batters, which means they hit batters with their pitch, are not necessarily the wildest pitchers. Sometimes in baseball, throwing the ball very close to a hitter is part of the strategy. And sometimes, well, those close pitches hit the batter instead of the bat. All-time great Walter Johnson of the Washington Senators dinged 205 hitters in his career.

SAD PITCHER STATS

Pitchers hate walks (also called bases on balls). Batters and opposing managers love them! Pitchers hate giving up hits, too. And they hate, hate, hate giving up home runs. Love 'em or hate 'em, these are the stats:

Most career walks allowed: Nolan Ryan, 2,795

Most walks allowed in a season: Bob Feller, 208 (1938)

Most hits allowed in a season: Joe McGinnity, 412 (1901)

Most career homers allowed: Jamie Moyer, 552

Most homers allowed in a season: Bert Blyleven, 50 (1986)

NOLAN RYAN

AVERAGES YOUR
GRANDPARENTS KNOW

These days, the way players are measured and evaluated is more complicated than it has ever been. Before we explore the data behind these newer measurements, let's first look at the classic ways stats are compiled for pitchers. These have been around since baseball began, and they are still important today.

EARNED RUN AVERAGE

A pitcher who lets the other team score has allowed a run. However, if his defense made errors—mistakes that would have otherwise been outs—the pitcher doesn't get the blame. Runs without errors are "earned" by the pitcher. Runs made with the help of errors are unearned. So, a key stat for pitchers is how many earned runs they give up. Baseball uses earned run average (ERA) to compare pitchers. The stat measures how many earned runs, on average, a pitcher gives up for every nine innings he pitches. A very good ERA is 3.00 or less. To figure this out, multiply earned runs (ER) by nine and divide by innings pitched (IP).

Here's the formula:

$$\frac{ER \times 9}{IP} = ERA$$

When he won the Cy Young Award in 2018, Jacob deGrom of the Mets gave up 41 earned runs in 217 IP. Here's how to figure his MLB-best ERA that season:

$$\begin{array}{c} 41 \text{ ER} \\ \times \quad 9 \\ \hline 369 \end{array}$$

$$\frac{369}{217} \rightarrow 217\sqrt{369} \qquad \boxed{1.70 \text{ ERA}}$$

JUSTIN VERLANDER

PENCIL POWER

Which of these pitchers has the better ERA?
JUSTIN VERLANDER: 60 ER, 214 IP
MILES MIKOLAS: 63 ER, 200 IP

ANSWER: Verlander, 2.52 to 2.84.

WINNING PERCENTAGE

For most of baseball history, the number of games won was considered the most important stat for pitchers. After all, the goal of the game is to win. A pitcher who won many more games than he lost is considered a star. A way to measure how much a player has won is by evaluating his winning percentage (WP; it's also called WPCT). You compare a pitcher's wins to the total number of games he won and lost. Win 6 out of 10, and you're probably an All-Star.

Here's the formula:

$$\frac{W}{W + L} = WPCT$$

In 1959, Roy Face won 18 games and lost only 1.

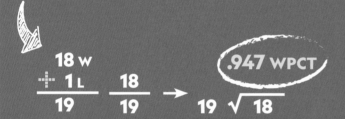

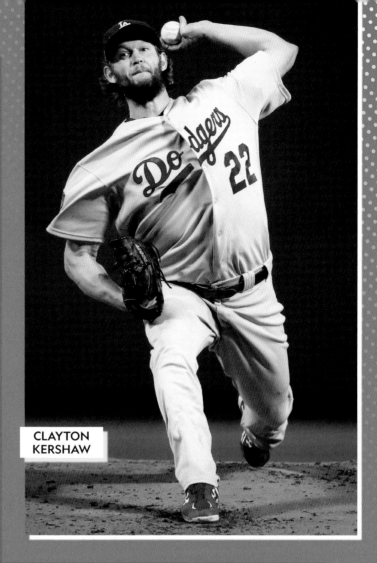

CLAYTON KERSHAW

CRACK THE WHIP

Pitchers do not want a batter to reach base, and record-keepers have always counted how often that occurs. In recent years, a popular way to calculate this is with WHIP: walks and hits per inning pitched. The lower the WHIP number, the better. A WHIP under one means you're really stingy about base runners! Remember that BB, or base on balls, is the same thing as a walk.

Here's the formula:

$$\frac{H + BB}{IP} = WHIP$$

In 2000, Boston Red Sox ace Pedro Martínez gave up 128 hits, and 32 bases on balls (BB) in 217 innings pitched.

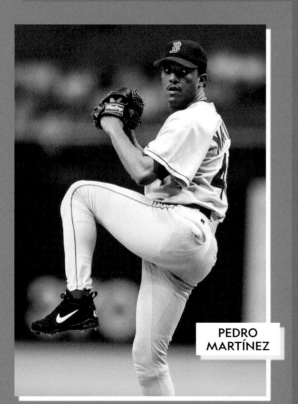

PEDRO MARTÍNEZ

AVERAGES YOUR *GRANDPARENTS* (PROBABLY) **DON'T KNOW**

There are a lot of stats you can calculate on your own. But for some of these stats, it's as if you need an advanced math degree to understand them! In fact, many MLB teams now employ professional mathematicians. Every MLB team has a special department that does nothing but crunch numbers. Called sports analytics, these calculations and stats are changing how players are selected and sometimes even how the game is played. Many of the new key stats revolve around pitching. Here are three:

ADJUSTED ERA+

If ERA measures how many earned runs a pitcher allows, how does that make it fair for every ballpark, since a fly ball in one place might be a homer in another? Enter the statheads. Adjusted ERA+ compares a pitcher's ERA to the whole league's ERA, and it makes mathematical adjustments based on the ballparks. ERA is one pitcher against his opponents; ERA+ compares that pitcher and his results to other pitchers but "evens the playing field," as MLB puts it.

Career Adjusted ERA+: Mariano Rivera, 205

Single-Season, Adjusted ERA+: Pedro Martínez, 291 (2000)

MARIANO RIVERA

CLAYTON KERSHAW

FIP

The statheads wanted a way to compare pitchers without any effect from fielding. That is, how well did the pitchers prevent homers, walks (BB), and HBP (hit by pitches), while also striking out a lot of hitters? This stat includes nothing that could be affected by how good or bad the fielders were. The result was a stat called fielding independent pitching (FIP). Once they had the formula (it's really complicated), the experts could apply it to every pitcher ever.

Best Career FIP: Ed Walsh, 2.018

Best Active Career FIP: Clayton Kershaw, 2.74

STRIKEOUT PERCENTAGE

One of the biggest reasons for coming up with new stats is to make the comparisons more fair. For instance, knowing that two pitchers each struck out about the same number of batters is fine, but it doesn't tell the whole story. What if one of them did it in twice as many innings or while facing far more batters? Just from K totals alone, you can't say who is a better strikeout pitcher. Bring on the calculator! Divide a pitcher's total strikeouts by the number of batters he has faced, and you get strikeout percentage (SP). Now you know who strikes players out more often.

Here's the formula:

$$\left(\frac{K}{BF} \right) 100 = SP$$

Hall of Fame lefty Randy "The Big Unit" Johnson had career totals of 4,875 strikeouts (K) and 17,067 batters faced (BF).

$$\frac{4875}{17067} \rightarrow 17067\sqrt{4875}^{.286} \rightarrow .286\ (100) = \boxed{28.6\ \text{SP}}$$

PENCIL POWER

Can you figure out these strikeout percentages?

Pedro Martínez for his 1999 best single-season mark: 313 K; 835 BF

Nolan Ryan, the Hall of Famer, for his 1973 season: 383 K; 1,355 BF

ANSWER: Martínez: 37.5; Ryan: 28.3

RANDY JOHNSON

FOLLOW THE **BALL**

Thanks to high-speed cameras, even higher-speed computers, and the amazing brains behind baseball technology, we get an enormous variety of information about every pitch. In the old days, pitchers had to rely on their coaches and their eyes. Today, they can see deep into the secret movement of baseballs. Speed is one thing, but movement is what really makes hitting difficult.

SPIN RATE

How fast a baseball is spinning affects how much it curves or drops (see Science Stuff on page 55). Using a tool called Trackman, teams can now measure how fast a pitch spins. Spin is measured in revolutions per minute (rpm). A revolution is one complete rotation of a sphere, which in this case is the baseball. The higher the rpm, the more spin a pitcher has put on the ball. The MLB average spin rate on a fastball is about 2,200 to 2,300 rpm. Studies have shown that batting averages go down when fastballs spin at rpms above 2,400. Experts theorize that the combination of high speed and higher spin make tracking the moving ball that much harder for batters.

Highest spin

Here are some of the highest average spin rates recorded by Statcast, which began tracking pitches in 2015:

Garrett Richards, Los Angeles Angels	2,688 rpm
Rich Hill, Los Angeles Dodgers	2,619 rpm
David Robertson, Philadelphia Phillies	2,586 rpm
Dellin Betances, New York Yankees	2,581 rpm
Kenley Jansen, Los Angeles Dodgers	2,562 rpm

GARRETT RICHARDS

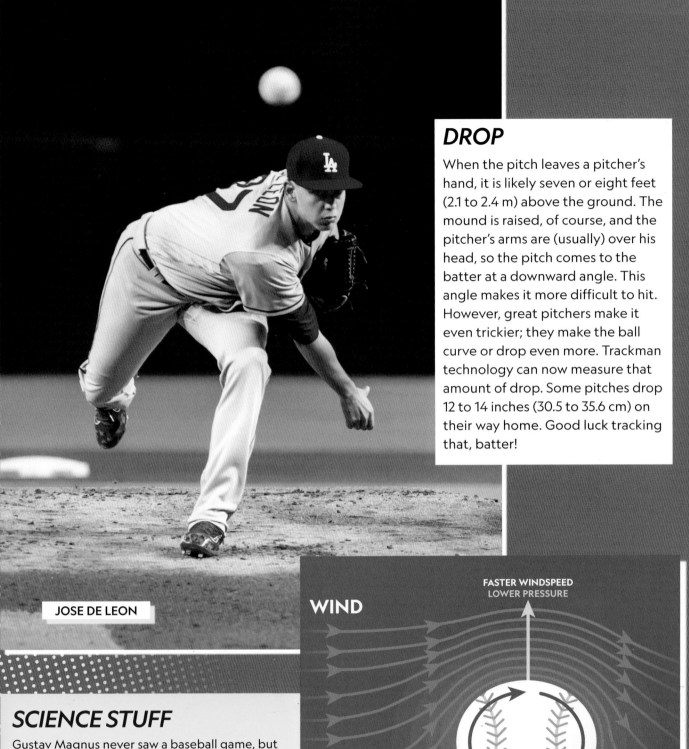

JOSE DE LEON

DROP

When the pitch leaves a pitcher's hand, it is likely seven or eight feet (2.1 to 2.4 m) above the ground. The mound is raised, of course, and the pitcher's arms are (usually) over his head, so the pitch comes to the batter at a downward angle. This angle makes it more difficult to hit. However, great pitchers make it even trickier; they make the ball curve or drop even more. Trackman technology can now measure that amount of drop. Some pitches drop 12 to 14 inches (30.5 to 35.6 cm) on their way home. Good luck tracking that, batter!

WIND

FASTER WINDSPEED
LOWER PRESSURE

SLOWER WINDSPEED
HIGHER PRESSURE

SCIENCE STUFF

Gustav Magnus never saw a baseball game, but his work is a part of each one. In 1853, the German scientist described the Magnus effect as the reason why curveballs curve. (The Magnus effect describes many things; the curve ball is only one of them.) The spin that a pitcher puts on the ball as he releases it makes the ball move in a curved path. The reason is that the spinning ball itself creates differing air pressure around the ball; the direction of the spin determines which side has lighter pressure—and that's the direction the spinning ball will move. The faster the rotation, the more the path will curve.

HIGH **SPEED!**

It's all about the speed! Speed is vital for a pitcher for the simple reason that it is harder to hit a fast pitch and easier to hit a slower pitch. Radar guns are measuring devices that have been used for a number of years to measure the speed of a pitch. They can track how fast an object is moving. Statcast and radar guns gather all the information they can about a pitcher's speed. This information is then displayed on scoreboards and television monitors for all of us to see.

SPEED KINGS

Here are the fastest pitchers ever recorded by a radar gun. Some pitchers in the days before we had this technology might have thrown faster; we'll never know for sure. Some of these players have thrown many pitches at these high speeds; for example, in 2016, Aroldis Chapman threw 24 pitches that topped 104 mph (167 km/h). This list includes each pitcher's fastest single pitch.

PITCHER, TEAM	SPEED IN MPH (KM/H)
Jordan Hicks, Cardinals	105.1 (169.1)
Aroldis Chapman, Yankees	105.1 (169.1)
Tayron Guerrero, Marlins	104 (167.4)
Mauricio Cabrera, Braves	103.8 (167.1)
Mark Wohlers, Braves	103 (165.8)
Tayron Guerrero, Marlins	102.9 (165.6)

HISTORY BY THE NUMBERS

Your grandparents may say, "Why isn't Nolan Ryan on that list? And what about Bob Feller?" Well, blame technology. Yes, baseball had some ways to measure pitch speed back then (Ryan pitched in the 1980s, and Feller debuted in the 1930s), but it was not nearly as accurate as our newer technology. Ryan hit 100.9 mph (162.4 km/h) once, and some math says that translates to 108 (173.8 km/h) on today's devices. Feller was said to reach 107 (172.2 km/h), but we can't be 100 percent sure. Statcast, which includes measurements from radar guns, cameras, and other gear, is the more accurate way to record speed now.

SCIENCE STUFF

Can pitchers throw even faster than they do now? Some scientists think they can't. The muscles of a pitcher's arm undergo enormous strain to throw at these high speeds. Doctors think that the physical limits of that strain have probably been reached. Though more pitchers than ever are throwing above 100 mph (161 km/h), they are not throwing that much above it. At a typical rate of improvement over many years, you'd expect a bigger jump, but that hasn't happened. It may never.

DIGIT-YOU-KNOW?

When facing a 95-mile-an-hour (153-km/h) fastball, a batter has less than a quarter of a second (.25 second) to decide whether to swing at the pitch or not. That goes up to just about a third of a second (0.3 second) on a curveball. Check this out:

- Time of average pitch to plate: 400 milliseconds
- Time to swing: 150 milliseconds
- Time to decide to swing: 250 milliseconds
  (that's as much time as it takes you to blink!)

MICHAEL CONFORTO

PITCHING HEROES

Who were the finest hurlers of the horsehide? Here are some of the top pitchers and the years they played. Who would you put on your list?

CHRISTY MATHEWSON

Years Active: 1900–16

In baseball's early days, players were often a rough-and-tumble bunch. Some players, though, helped change what fans thought of baseball players in general. Mathewson was known for being very polite. People say he acted more like a gentleman than a tough guy. He was also a spectacular pitcher. Mathewson led the NL in ERA five times and helped the New York Giants win the 1905 World Series.

SANDY KOUFAX

Years Active: 1955–66

Though his career lasted only 12 years, Koufax is often considered the best pitcher of all time. The lefty threw four no-hitters, including a perfect game, and won three Cy Young Awards. He led the NL in ERA for five straight years and in strikeouts four years. In 1965, he set the then-record for 382 strikeouts. Koufax had an incredible fastball and a knee-buckling curve— meaning a pitch that curves so much, batters' knees buckle because they think the ball is going to hit them.

SATCHEL PAIGE

Years Active: 1948–53, 1965

Paige only pitched during some of six MLB seasons, but he was one of the game's greatest hurlers. He threw a tremendous fastball but spent most of his Hall of Fame career in the Negro Leagues. The Negro Leagues—named using a term that was generally accepted for the time but is now considered offensive—formed in the first half of the 20th century. It consisted of African-American pros who were unfairly banned from playing in MLB because of their race. Despite being forced to play in this separate league because of racist rules, Paige "barnstormed" the country, playing exhibition games against pro and amateur teams. He pitched a game in the majors when he was 59!

BOB GIBSON

Years Active: 1959–75

Gibson dominated the NL in the 1960s. His 1.12 ERA in 1968 was the best in the 20th century since World War I. He led the St. Louis Cardinals to three World Series championships, including winning three games for them in the 1967 Series.

PEDRO MARTÍNEZ

Years Active: 1992–2009

Martínez developed a high-speed fastball and a super slider (a slider is a breaking pitch that moves side to side and down). His best seasons included 1999, when he won the pitching Triple Crown (leading the league in ERA, wins, and strikeouts). That was one of five seasons he was the ERA champ. He also won three Cy Young Awards.

MAX SCHERZER

Years Active: 2008–present

This Washington Nationals righty is one of today's best pitchers. A three-time Cy Young winner and four-time strikeout champ, Scherzer is fast and furious. He combines power with great control; he has had a WHIP over 1.00 just once since 2014.

TRY *THIS!*

Keep Score

The big digital scoreboard at a ballpark is packed with numbers and names. It shows who is up, what the score is, and the count for balls and strikes per batter. But you don't need a digital device to keep score. Using a grid of batters and innings, fans and baseball writers record every event in the game. They use a code of numbers and symbols to quickly and simply mark down the information. Some of these grids use a little diamond symbol as a place to record where the base runners went. Others check boxes to keep track of balls and strikes.

WHAT YOU NEED:

- Paper
- A pencil

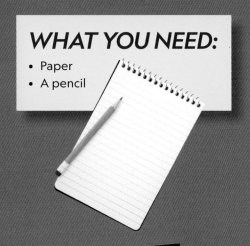

Team:				vs						at			End Time:			Time of Game:		
Date:			Start Time:											Scorer:				
Weather:												AB	R	H	RBI	E	
Umpires:																	

#	Player	Pos	1	2	3	4	5	6	7	8	9	10

Runs

S U M S   Pitcher   BB

In the score sheet above, J. Gordon plays right field and wears jersey number 8. He batted first in the lineup and walked. When J. Clendening grounded out to shortstop, Gordon advanced to second on fielder's choice. He was stranded there when Davidson struck out. In third inning, Gordon grounded out when the third baseman (5) threw to the first baseman (3).

Team:		vs		
Date: 4-15-20		Start Time: 1:05		
Weather: nice				
Umpires: F. Morty				

#	Player	Pos	1	2	3	4	5
8	J. Gordon / sub	RF	FC / BB		5-3		
13	J. Csiszar / sub	1B	F8		HR		
24	J. Clendening / sub	CF	6-3		6-4 / E4		
11	G. Davidson / sub	SS	K		6-4-3		
10	D. Sugiyama / sub	C		2B	SB / HBA		
30	D. Ginsberg / sub	3B		RBI / 1B	3B		

The lists here show the position codes and some of the event codes that can be used for these scorecards. Check out the example scorecard on page 60. Then try to make your own grid (or ask an adult to help you find one online) to keep score of a real game.

POSITIONS

LETTER CODE	NUMBER CODE	POSITION
P	1	Pitcher
C	2	Catcher
1B	3	First base
2B	4	Second base
3B	5	Third base
SS	6	Shortstop
LF	7	Left field
CF	8	Center field
RF	9	Right field

Note: 1B means a single, and it also means the defensive position first base.

Make Your Own

Feeling creative? Instead of using the symbols provided here, make up your own! For example, instead of 1B for a single, you could draw a "—". For a double, draw two lines, one over the other, like an equal sign.

SYMBOLS

These are the abbreviations most frequently used to keep score.

SYMBOL	EVENT
1B, 2B, 3B	single, double, triple
BB	walk
E	error, followed by the number of the position that made it
HR	home run
F	fly out
FC	fielder's choice
SB	stolen base
K	strikeout swinging
ʞ	strikeout looking, when the umpire calls the batter out on a third strike instead of the batter swinging and missing
SF	sacrifice fly
WP	wild pitch, when a pitch eludes the catcher and lets base runners run to the next base while the catcher runs after the ball

Note: If an out is recorded with help from more than one player, mark which players touched the ball and in what order. For example, a ball hit to the shortstop and then thrown to first base is marked as "6-3."

Test Your Skills:

How would you record the at bats of these four batters?

Batter A: ground ball to the third baseman, who throws to first for the out

Batter B: a "called" strike three (which means he didn't swing)

Batter C: a double

Batter D: a long fly ball that is caught by the right fielder

ANSWERS: A: 5-3; B: backward K; C: 2B; D: F9

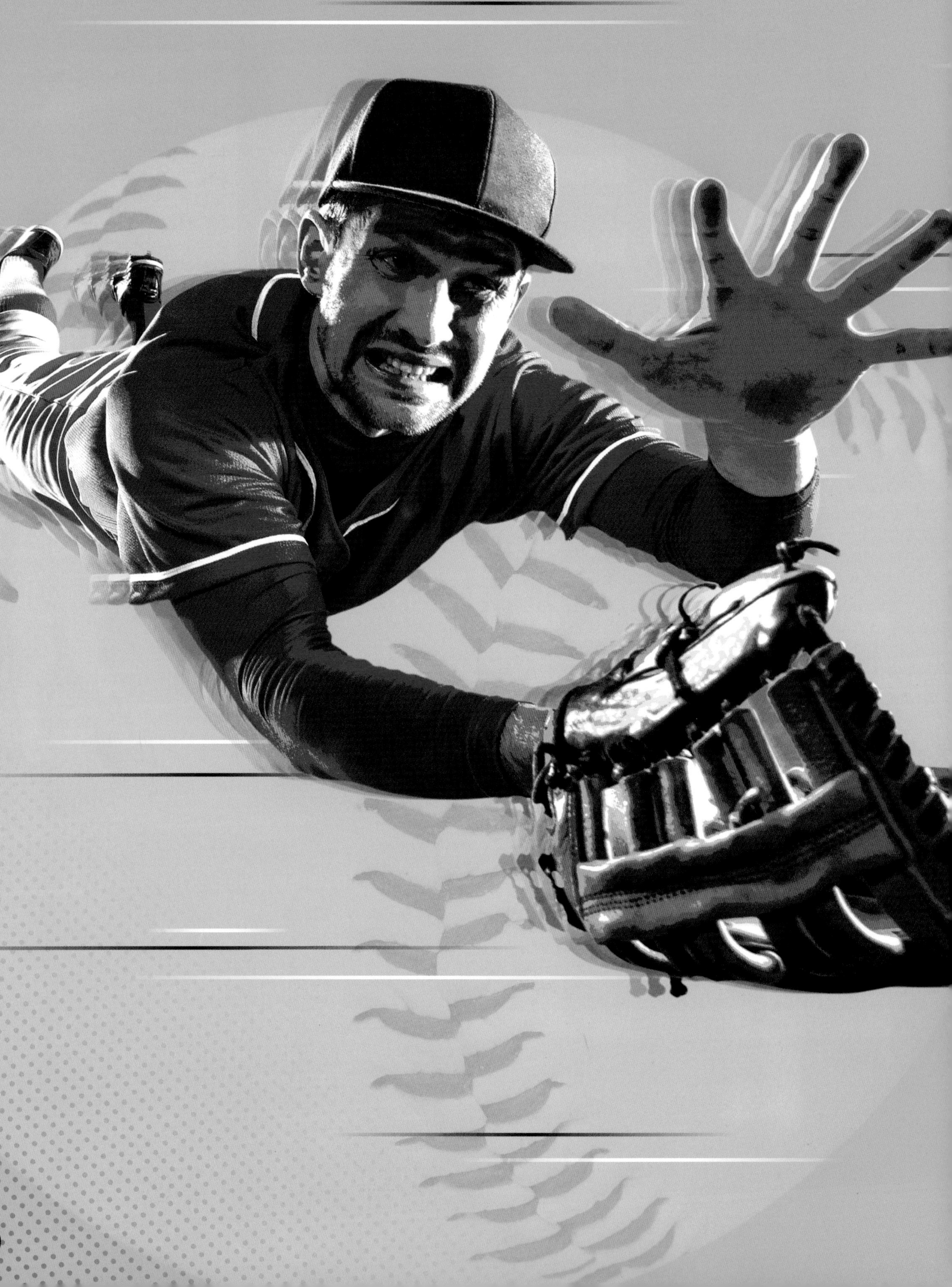

CHAPTER FOUR

BASERUNNING AND FIELDING

O ften, it seems like pitchers and home run hitters are the stars of the show. But baseball wouldn't be baseball without fielding and baserunning. Fielding is any handling of the ball in the field after it's hit by the batter—you know, catching and throwing. On the bases, you can steal and show off your speed. In the field, you can record outs (hooray!) and make errors (boo!). Let's check out the stats for runners and fielders.

DIGIT-YOU-KNOW?

When the game was first being played, no one used baseball gloves. When gloves first appeared on the field, in the early 1870s, they were nothing more than smushy, short-fingered, floppy things. Players even left them on the field between innings. Yes, that meant that fielders sometimes had to step over their opponents' gloves lying in the grass during a play! It wasn't until the 1960s that gloves increased in size. Players began wearing oversize, basketlike gloves. MLB eventually put rules in place that limit the length of the glove to 13 inches (33 cm). The width of the glove cannot exceed 7.75 inches (19.7 cm). Catcher's mitts and first baseman's gloves are specialized and have different dimensions.

GAME OF **SPEED** AND **SCIENCE**

On the field, speed is an important tool. It can be the difference between reaching a fly ball and the ball landing in the grass. Speed is vital on the basepaths, too. As soon as a batter becomes a runner, he has to hustle to first base and hopefully then also make it around the bases. Of course, stealing bases only works if you are as quick as a flash!

SPRINT SPEED

Baseball scouts carry a stopwatch. For every batter they evaluate, they time the batter's speed from the instant he hits the ball to the moment he steps on first. The less time that takes, the better. The difference between a fast runner, an average runner, and a slow runner is only fractions of a second. A great MLB runner can sprint from home to first in about 3.5 seconds. A slow one takes perhaps a second longer. Another way to measure sprint speed is feet per second, which is what Statcast precisely captures.

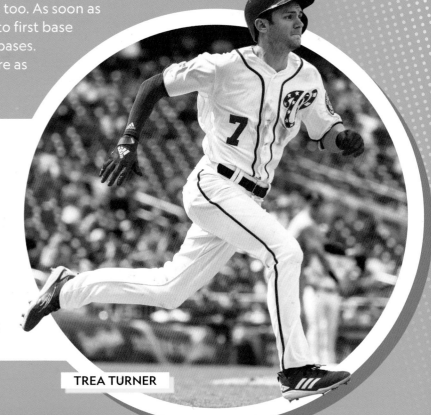

TREA TURNER

SPRINT SPEED

30.8 feet/sec (9.4 m/sec)
(Tim Locastro, Arizona Diamondbacks)

30.4 feet/sec (9.3 m/sec)
(Trea Turner, Washington Nationals)

30.3 feet/sec (9.2 m/sec)
(Byron Buxton, Minnesota Twins)

FIRST TO THIRD

Did you know that baseball players use science to run from first to third? Getting from first base to third base on a single by a teammate can change a game. To make the play work, runners need to get a good lead during the pitch and then sprint and reach top speed quickly. They then need to make a quick turn at second base. So, where does the science come in? The key is in the curve. Usually, the fastest way from one point to another is a straight line. But players don't just run straight to second and then straight to third, because that would mean they would need to nearly stop to change direction so drastically, which would actually slow them down. Instead, they have to find a path that lets them touch second base while not losing any of their speed. They also need to lean their body inward to help stay on that curved path. The lean balances out the centrifugal force pushing the runner's body outward as he runs along a curved path. A good runner might run 200 or more feet (61 m) to cover a base-to-base-to-base distance of 180 feet (54.9 m).

RUNNING ARC

SHOHEI OHTANI

STEALING

The baseball diamond is one of the few places in the world where stealing something is considered a good thing. What do players steal? Bases, of course! Once a runner is on base, he can try to run to the next base during any pitch to the plate. If he is not tagged out, he has "stolen" the base. Here's a look at some key stolen-base numbers.

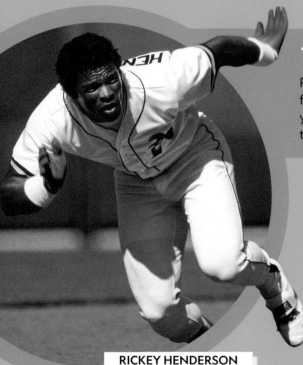

RICKEY HENDERSON

THE BEST

Players with the most stolen bases (SB) are also among the best for all-around skill. Why? Before you get the chance to show off your speed by stealing bases, you first have to get on base. So that means being a great hitter and a fast runner, too.

CAREER STOLEN BASE RECORD:
RICKEY HENDERSON
(1979–2003) **1,406**

THE VANISHING STEAL

In terms of baseball strategy, coaches don't always agree that stealing bases will help secure a win. These days, the total number of steals is down from the early days of baseball. At other times in baseball history, the steal was hugely popular.

YEARS OF THE STEALS

Who swiped the most bags (slang for bases) in a year? The 1970s and 1980s were prime time for some of baseball's biggest thieves, so most of the single-year bests are from that era.

SINGLE-SEASON STOLEN BASE LEADERS

RICKEY HENDERSON, Oakland Athletics, 130, 1982

LOU BROCK, St. Louis Cardinals, 118, 1974

VINCE COLEMAN, St. Louis Cardinals, 110, 1985

VINCE COLEMAN

STOLEN BASES BY YEAR

Here's a comparison between the years in each decade that had the highest average number of steals per game. The per-game average provides the most reliable comparison because the number of teams has changed over the years—from 16 in the early days to 30 today.

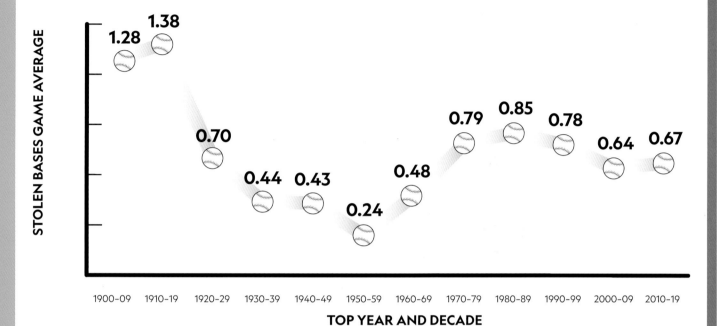

STOLEN BASES GAME AVERAGE

1.28   1.38   0.70   0.44   0.43   0.24   0.48   0.79   0.85   0.78   0.64   0.67

1900-09   1910-19   1920-29   1930-39   1940-49   1950-59   1960-69   1970-79   1980-89   1990-99   2000-09   2010-19

TOP YEAR AND DECADE

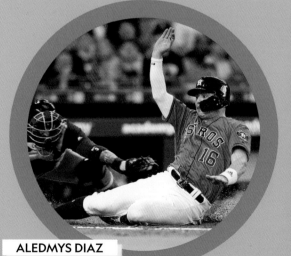

ALEDMYS DIAZ

STEALING HOME

Few plays in baseball are more exciting than a steal of home plate. These players stole home more often than any others.

PLAYER (Years of Career)	STEALS HOME
Ty Cobb (1905–28)	54
Max Carey (1910–29)	33
George Burns (1911–25)	28
Honus Wagner (1897–1917)	27

HISTORY BY THE NUMBERS

"Sliding" Billy Hamilton (1888–1901) played during an era in which steals were a huge part of the game. Few homers were hit, so teams used every advantage to move around the bases. In 2019, one of the top base stealers was also named Billy Hamilton, who had been in MLB since 2013! This speedster had four seasons in a row (2014–17) with 50 or more steals.

BILLY HAMILTON

WHEN TO **STEAL A BASE**

Teams today have special tools to help them decide when it's likely the safest moment to try to steal a base. It all starts with a stopwatch.

1 Get to first base. With a runner on first base, the calculations begin. The first thing to know is approximately how long it takes that runner to go from first to second. That's called the running time. The fastest runners need about 3.5 seconds to run from first to second.

2 The first-base coach carries a stopwatch. As the pitcher throws to home plate, the coach uses the watch to see how long it takes from when the pitcher starts throwing to when the ball hits the catcher's mitt. This takes perhaps 1.3 to 1.5 seconds.

BILLY HAMILTON

3 Teams study their opponents to find out this third number. Called "pop time," this is the measurement of how long a catcher takes to get the ball from his glove to his teammate at second base. As an example, J.T. Realmuto of the Philadelphia Phillies averaged 1.88 seconds of pop time in 2019; that was best in the majors. The 50th best pop time was still only 2.03 seconds, so we're talking about a pretty tiny window here!

STAT STORY

Why "pop" time? The name come from the sounds the ball makes when it smacks into the catcher's glove and then whaps into the fielder's glove!

CHANCE SISCO

TIM ANDERSON

ADALBERTO MONDESI

4

Add time to the plate to pop time and compare it to running time. If the running time is less, go for the steal!

Here's the formula:

Time to plate + Pop time
If the sum is greater than (>) running time, go for the steal.

Let's put it all together. J.T. Realmuto of the Phillies is the catcher for Aaron Nola. Speedy Billy Hamilton is on first for the Atlanta Braves. Combine Nola's time-to-plate of 1.4 seconds and Realmuto's pop time of 1.8 seconds to Hamilton's first-to-second running time of 3.3. Should he run?

1.4 time to plate
+ 1.8 pop time
3.2

Is 3.2 > 3.3?

No, don't go for the steal. It will be a very close play!

PENCIL POWER

Decide which of these runners you would let try to steal a base!

PLAYER (running time)	TIME TO PLATE	POP TIME
A (3.0)	1.2	2.0
B (3.3)	1.4	2.1
C (3.6)	1.5	2.0

ANSWER: Tell A and B to attempt a steal. C should wait.

COUNTING *ASSISTS* AND *PUTOUTS*

It's time to play defense. That's what the players in the field are doing. When the batter hits the ball, the defense works to make an out or keep the batter from advancing around the bases. They do that by catching the ball wherever it's hit and throwing it to a teammate. But don't get all "put out"—we'll count here, too!

PUTOUTS

The object of the defense is to get the batter out. Each time a runner is forced or tagged out, the defensive player who makes that play earns a "putout" (PO). A force play is one in which the fielder tags the base ahead of the charging runner to record the out. On a tag play, the ball (or the glove with a ball in it) has to touch the runner before he can touch the base. Not surprisingly, first basemen usually get the most POs, since more plays end there than at other bases. Catchers record the second most POs, since they earn one for catching strikeouts. A fielder gets a PO for catching a fly ball or a line drive.

EDWIN ENCARNACION

ASSISTS

The first baseman making the putout needs help. When a player throws the ball to the player with the putout, the throwing player earns an assist. As you might expect, infielders make the most assists, since most of the ground balls are hit to them.

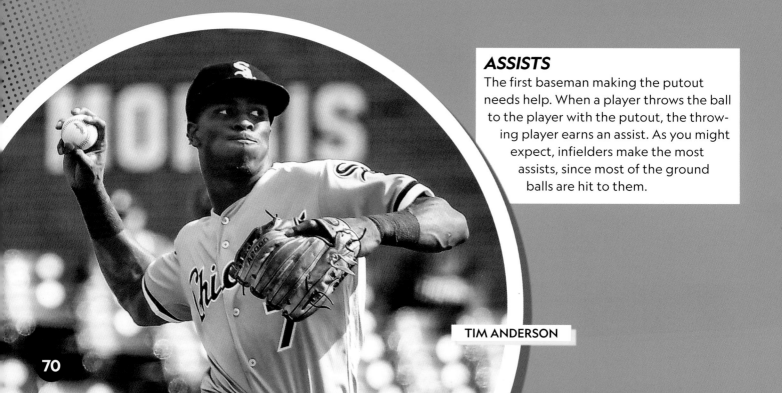

TIM ANDERSON

IVAN RODRIGUEZ

AROUND THE DIAMOND

Here are the all-time leaders in assists and putouts for each of the nine positions on the diamond. Note that the outfield totals are only from 1908 onward because separate records for each position were not kept until then.

CAREER ASSISTS

CAREER PUTOUTS

RF
Harry Hooper 332
Paul Waner 4,740

CF
Tris Speaker 444
Willie Mays 7,022

2B
Eddie Collins 7,630
Eddie Collins 6,526

1B
Eddie Murray 1,865
Jake Beckley 23,755

SS
Ozzie Smith 8,375
Rabbit Maranville 5,139

P
Cy Young 2,014
Greg Maddux 546

LF
Zack Wheat 233
Barry Bonds 5,225

3B
Brooks Robinson 6,205
Brooks Robinson 2,697

C
Deacon Maguire 1,860
Ivan Rodriguez 14,864

OOPS! COUNTING ERRORS

There is one type of stat that no one wants on their scorebook. We're talking about errors. When a fielder drops a fly ball or misses a grounder or when he throws the ball past his teammate, and when he gets the big E. Not surprisingly, infielders make more errors than outfielders, simply because they have more chances to catch the ball—more balls are hit to infielders than to outfielders. Here are the career and single-season error leaders at each position— hope that none of your favorite players are on this list!

Defense was much harder in the early 20th century because of smaller, less sophisticated gloves (or none at all) and because the game was often played on rather rough fields. As a result, this chart uses the post-1901 "modern era" records. Outfield records are since 1908.

Making a lot of errors in your career is only possible if you're really good at hitting. Otherwise, it's not likely your team will keep you on for long. As evidence, each player on this all-time errors list with an asterisk by his name is in the Baseball Hall of Fame. You can make up for errors by being a terrific hitter!

POSITION	CAREER	SINGLE-SEASON
C	Ivey Wingo, 234	Oscar Stanage, 41 (1911)
P	Cy Young,* 146	Doc Newton, 18 (1901)
1B	Hal Chase, 402	Jerry Freeman, 41 (1908)
2B	Nap Lajoie,* 451	Kid Gleason, 64 (1901)
3B	Jimmy Collins,* 465	Tommy Leach, 25 (1903)
SS	Bill Dahlen, 975	John Gochnaur, 98 (1903)
LF	Goose Goslin* and Zack Wheat, 184 (tie)	Ken Williams, 26 (1921)
CF	Tris Speaker,* 226	Clyde Milan, 25 (1912)
RF	Harry Hooper,* 142	Chuck Klein,* 23 (1936)

STAT STORY

At each MLB game, one baseball expert serves as the official scorer. This person watches every play very carefully. The scorer decides whether a play is a hit or an error. He or she then reports that to the media covering the game. This ruling also appears on the scoreboard. If a third baseman missed a ground ball, for instance, the scorer would put E-5 on the scoreboard. (Why 5? See page 61.)

JERRY HAIRSTON, JR., OF THE NEW YORK YANKEES MAKES AN ERROR IN A GAME AGAINST THE BALTIMORE ORIOLES.

TWICE AS NICE AND **TRIPLE THE FUN**

What's better for a fielding team than getting a batter out? Getting two players out at the same time. What about three players? Even better! The double play, also called the "pitcher's best friend," is when the defense gets two outs on a single hit. A triple play, which is much less likely, is three outs on one ball.

MICKEY VERNON

DOUBLE PLAY KINGS

Here are the infielders who were involved in the most double plays as fielders.

1B	Mickey Vernon, 2,044
2B	Bill Mazeroski, 1,706
3B	Brooks Robinson, 618
SS	Omar Vizquel, 1,734

PENCIL POWER

Remember how you learned to keep score? How would you record these double plays using the codes on page 61?

1. With a runner on first base, a ground ball is hit to the shortstop. He throws to the second baseman who steps on second. Then the second baseman throws to the first baseman to get the second out.

2. A "comebacker" is hit to the pitcher with a man on first and second. He turns and fires the ball to the shortstop, who is covering second base. The shortstop then throws to first.

3. A fly ball is hit to the right fielder. He catches it and throws to third base. His throw beats the runner trying to advance from second base. Out at third!

ANSWERS: 1. 6-4-3, 2. 1-6-3, 3. 9-5.

DIGIT-YOU-KNOW?

There are actually 17 ways to turn a double play, but the vast majority of them happen on the infield on ground balls. The classic 6-4-3 (shortstop to second to first) accounts for about 30 percent of double plays on average, with 4-6-3 making up about 25 percent.

LUIS JIMENEZ

UNASSISTED TRIPLE PLAY

One of the rarest feats in baseball is the unassisted triple play. These occur when one fielder makes all three putouts on the same play. Of course, there have to be at least two runners on base and nobody out for this even to be possible. Then, it's a matter of skill and luck to find the fielder, the ball, and the two base runners in just the right places. Through 2019, there have been a total of only 15 of these plays.

TROY TULOWITZKI WRAPS UP ONE OF BASEBALL'S RAREST PLAYS.

HISTORY BY THE NUMBERS

The name Bill Wambsganss may otherwise be lost to history if not for what he did on October 10, 1920. That's the day that the Cleveland Indians second baseman nabbed a line drive, stepped on second to record a second out, and tagged a charging runner for the third out. His unassisted triple play was extra special because it was the only one ever to occur in a World Series game.

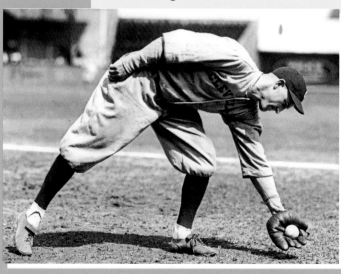

STAT STARS

Infielders don't get all the double play (DP) glory. Outfielders can help with a DP by catching a fly ball and then throwing out a runner. The great center fielder Tris Speaker holds the record for such plays, with 146 in his Hall of Fame career. He played from 1907 to 1928, mostly for the Boston Red Sox and Cleveland Indians.

GLOVE **MATH**

AARON JUDGE

How do you compare fielders? Because some fielding positions get a lot more chances than others, it's not fair to compare each position using the same set of measurements. For example, a first baseman will certainly get a lot more putouts than a right fielder, but that doesn't make 1Bs better than RFs. So instead of comparing how many outs players get in the field, let's look at how well they do when they have a chance to make a play.

FIELDING AVERAGE

To find fielding average (FA), which is also called fielding percentage, you need to know the number of errors a player made, along with the number of assists and putouts, also known collectively as "chances." By looking at these stats, we can find out how successful a fielder was. That is, how often did he do the job right and avoid making an error?

Total the assists (A) and putouts (PO) and then divide that number by the total of assists, putouts, and errors (E), or total chances. The result is the fielding average, or fielding percentage. An average of 1.000 means the player made zero errors!

Here's the formula: $$\frac{A + PO}{A + PO + E} = FA$$

NOLAN ARENADO

Colorado third baseman Nolan Arenado won his eighth Gold Glove for fielding excellence in 2019. He had 337 assists, 111 putouts, and only 9 errors.

$$+ \frac{337 \text{ assists}}{111 \text{ pullouts}} = 448 \qquad + \frac{337 \text{ assists}}{\begin{array}{c}111 \text{ pullouts}\\9 \text{ errors}\end{array}} = 457 \qquad \frac{448}{457} \rightarrow 457 \sqrt{448} = .980 \text{ FA}$$

PENCIL POWER

Can you figure out the fielding averages of shortstops Trevor Story and the great Hall of Famer Ozzie Smith?

TREVOR STORY	OZZIE SMITH
(in the 2019 season)	(career)
416 assists	8,375 assists
182 putouts	4,249 putouts
8 errors	281 errors

ANSWER: Trevor Story .987; Ozzie Smith .978

OZZIE SMITH

CASEY KOTCHMAN

ALL-TIME FIELDING AVERAGE LEADERS

P	5 pitchers,* 1.000
C	Chris Snyder, .998
1B	Casey Kotchman, .997
2B	Plácido Polanco, .993
3B	Plácido Polanco, .983
SS	Omar Vizquel, .985
RF	Nick Markakis, .994
CF	Darin Erstad, .997
LF	Brian Downing, .995

*Jim Bullinger, Josh Collmenter, Paul Mitchell, Luis Vizcaino, and Paul Wagner

STAT STORY

The top fielder at each position in the AL and NL is given the Gold Glove at the end of the season. Managers and coaches vote to select the winner. The award began in 1957. The award itself is really a shiny gold glove!

MOST GOLD GLOVES BY POSITION

C	Ivan Rodriguez, 13
P	Greg Maddux, 18
1B	Keith Hernandez, 11
2B	Roberto Alomar, 10
3B	Brooks Robinson, 16
SS	Ozzie Smith, 13
OF	Roberto Clemente, Willie Mays, 12

Find the Best Thief

Want to find out who among your friends is best at stealing bases?

WHAT YOU NEED:

- Stopwatch
- Baseball diamond (with bases)
- Friends
- Paper and pen

1 Grab a group of friends.

Set up bases 90 feet (27.4 m) apart, the distance used in big-league diamonds. If you need to estimate 90 feet, simply start walking and count out 90 steps, or paces.

Time each person running from first to second. Write it down.

2 Time each person's pitch to home plate. Write it down.

Using your results, and using an MLB pop time of 2.03, do the math: Add pitch time to pop time. Compare it to the time from first to second (see page 68). Should you have that runner try to steal second?

SPEEDIEST BASE RUNNER

While you are out on the field with your stopwatch and friends, why not also find out who is the fastest base runner?

1. Time each friend running a straight line from home to first. Write it down.
2. Time each friend running the curved path from first to third. Write it down.
3. Make a chart of your times.
4. Compare the two sets of numbers. Who was best from home to first? Who was fastest from first to third? It might not be the same person!

CHAPTER FIVE

SUPER

STATS

In baseball today, sabermetrics rule. Say what? Sabermetrics are the complicated statistics that look at players, teams, and the game itself. Another way to describe how we look at this data is called analytics. Whatever you call it, these new stats are revolutionizing baseball. MLB teams each employ a group of experts who know more about computers, math, and stats than they do about how to throw a curveball or steal a base. These dataheads gather the zillions of numbers generated by every pitch, hit, run, game, series, season, and more. They run these numbers through advanced math calculations and try to see patterns and outcomes. Why all this work? By using math, baseball teams hope to make better decisions about which players to sign and what strategies to use, and of course, find new ways to win.

STAT STORY

Why "sabermetrics" when there is no saber, or sword, in baseball? The nickname comes from the initials of the Society for American Baseball Research (SABR, get it?). Founded in 1971, this private group is devoted to finding out every single thing possible about baseball stats, history, and players. SABR has more than 6,000 statheads, er, members.

THE WINNING NUMBER

Hitting, playing defense, baserunning—each player does so many different things in so many positions. How can you possibly compare players across a team? Until recently, there was not one stat that could tell you everything. Then, along came WAR: wins above replacement. Using data on hitting, defense, and baserunning, statisticians create a single number. That number tells how many wins per season a player accounts for, compared to an average player from the same position.

WAR can be used to compare pitchers as well as hitters. Much more than batting average or fielding average, WAR is seen among experts as the best way to compare players. An MLB player's WAR score is usually in the 2 to 6 range, with a handful of top players exceeding 10. We can also use the WAR stats from each player's different seasons to create a career WAR number.

ON THE SCALE

For single-season WAR, teams use this scale as a rough guide to what the numbers mean. The numbers are each player's WAR score. For example, Houston shortstop Alex Bregman had a 9.1 WAR score in 2019; he was an All-Star and among the top vote-getters for the AL MVP award. His teammate, catcher Robinson Chirinos, had a WAR of 3.8. He was a solid player, but not an All-Star.

0	Replacement-level player
0 to 2	Reserve/backup
2 up	Starting position player
5 up	All-Star level
8 up	MVP level

ALEX BREGMAN LEAPS OVER A SLIDING BRIAN GOODWIN.

CAREER WAR HITTERS:

Babe Ruth	182.5
Barry Bonds	162.8
Willie Mays	156.4

CAREER WAR PITCHERS:

Cy Young	163.8
Walter Johnson	151.6
Roger Clemens	138.7

SINGLE-SEASON
(SINCE 1901)
WAR PITCHERS:

Walter Johnson	15.1 (1913)
Walter Johnson	13.2 (1912)
Cy Young	12.6 (1901)

SINGLE-SEASON WAR HITTERS

Babe Ruth	14.1 (1923)
Babe Ruth	12.8 (1921)
Babe Ruth	12.5 (1927)
Carl Yastrzemski	12.5 (1967)

CARL YASTRZEMSKI

DIGIT-YOU-KNOW?

There is one basic WAR calculation. However, three companies each use slightly different data in doing their math. Here we're using the numbers that are most often seen in sports pages. Here's how MLB.com writes out the actual WAR calculation (take a deep breath!):

WAR = The number of runs above average a player earns through his batting, baserunning, and fielding + adjustment for position + adjustment for league + the number of runs provided by a replacement-level player / runs per win

So, yes, it's very complicated, and most of the computations are done by computers. Don't worry, though—you don't have to understand the math behind this stat to understand *why* it has become so important. It's the result that matters, not the very complex formula used to create those results.

SUPREME SLUGGERS

Remember on-base percentage and slugging average (page 30)? In the last few years, these two stats have become more important when evaluating a player's skill. Statheads combined them to create another new stat called OPS, which stands for on-base percentage plus slugging average.

Normally, you would not add two percentages to get a new one. But since this is baseball, and not math class, that's just how the statheads decided OPS should work.

Why do we need OPS? The number-crunchers determined that how often a player gets on base and how many bases his hits earn are the best ways to measure success.

Here's the formula:

OBP + SA = OPS

Babe Ruth has the highest career OPS ever. His career on-base percentage (OBP) is .474, and his slugging average (SA) is .690, which makes his OPS 1.164.

.474 OBP
+ .690 SA
——————
1. 164 OPS

Red Sox slugger J.D. Martinez has a career OBP of .357 and a career SA of .537. What is his OPS?

ANSWER: .894

OPS+

Want to get even more complicated? OPS+ takes a player's OPS and then factors in the ballparks in which he plays and his league (AL or NL). The math gets pretty tricky, but the result is a number that compares not only a player's hitting skills, but also takes into account how ballparks and opponents affect the number.

PENCIL POWER

Which of these sluggers has the highest OPS?

A: .330 OBP
.468 SA

B: .390 OBP
.410 SA

C: .360 OPB
.425 SA

ANSWER: It's close, but it's Player B by an eyelash!

ALL-TIME CAREER OPS LEADERS

Babe Ruth	1.164
Ted Williams	1.116
Lou Gehrig	1.08
Barry Bonds	1.051
Jimmie Foxx	1.038
Hank Greenberg	1.017
Rogers Hornsby	1.010
Mike Trout	.999
Manny Ramirez	.996
Mark McGwire	.982

MIKE TROUT

SAY *WHAT?*

Say BABIP, VORP, and LIPS aloud and your friends may think you are speaking an alien language. But these are the names of more mind-blowing sabermetric stats being used in baseball.

BABIP

Batting average on balls in play (BABIP) calculates how often a player gets a hit against each time he puts the ball into play on the field—minus home runs. Good defense will lower a batter's BABIP, while bad defense will raise it. Luck helps, too. If teams see an average player's BABIP shoot up one season, they know it's probably not because he's suddenly a great hitter. He might simply be lucky that year!

Here's the formula:

$$\frac{H - HR}{AB - K - HR + SF} = BABIP$$

DJ LeMahieu of the Yankees had a great season in 2019. A big reason was his very high BABIP. In 602 at bats, he got 197 hits, including 26 homers. He struck out 90 times and had 4 sacrifice flies.

197 hits		602 at bats		512		486	
− 26 homers		− 90 strikeouts		− 26 homers		+ 4 sacrifices	
171		**512**		**486**		**490**	

Need a quick refresher? Check out the list of abbreviations on page 124.

$$\frac{171}{490} \rightarrow 490\sqrt{171}$$

.349 BABIP

DJ LEMAHIEU

PENCIL POWER

San Diego's slugging third baseman Manny Machado did not have a huge BABIP in 2019. See if you can figure it out. He had 150 H and 32 HR with 587 AB. He struck out 128 times (K) and had 3 sacrifice flies (SF).

ANSWER: .274 BABIP

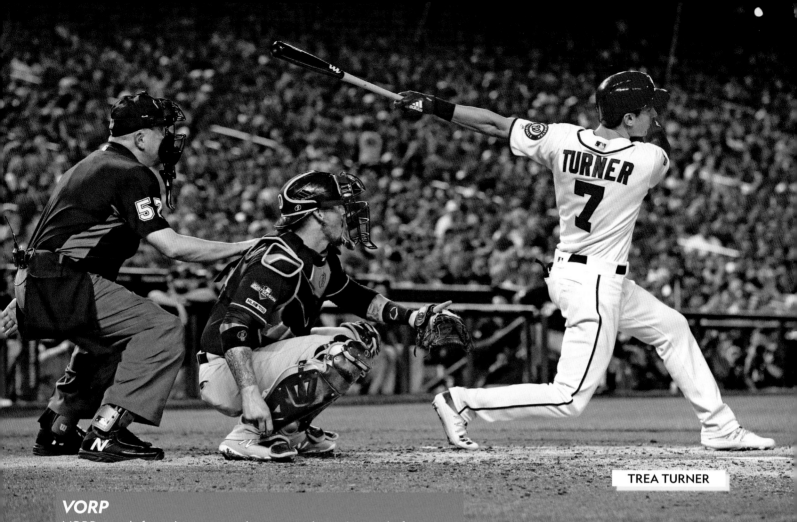

TREA TURNER

VORP

VORP stands for value over replacement player. Instead of measuring how many wins a new player will help a team earn, VORP measures how many more runs a player could contribute to his team versus what an average replacement player would do.

HISTORY BY THE NUMBERS

In the 1970s, Bill James worked as a night watchman. His late-night security shift had very little going on, and he found himself with extra time on his hands, which he used to review baseball stats for hours and hours. He started looking at new ways of working with the data. Over time, he became a well-known expert. He is the author of many important books and has created stats still in use today. James has since been hired by some MLB teams to help create their analytics departments.

LIPS

Which batters can make a big hit when their teams need them most? Can a stat really predict that? LIPS, late-inning pressure situations, can do just that. Coming up with the LIPS number involves calculating what the batter did and how that compares to league averages in similar spots. It's complicated. MLB says the following are the key moments when hitters need to come through for their team:

• In the seventh inning or later
• Their team is behind by three runs or fewer
• The teams are tied
• Their team is only ahead by one
• Their team is down by four and the bases are loaded

DIGITS ON DEFENSE

Don't worry, sabermetrics cover fielding, too! Defensive runs saved (DRS) has become one of the go-to standards for comparing fielders. The idea of DRS stats is to figure out how many runs a player prevented from scoring by tracking what he's done on the field. A similar stat is ultimate zone rating (UZR), which uses a slightly different calculation.

THE SHIFT IS ON!

Based on all the data we now have available, MLB clubs move their fielders around to protect the areas where a hitter most often hits the ball. These "shifts" try to put more fielders into a batter's best hitting spots. The shortstop might move closer to first base, for example. The third baseman might move all the way to the grass between first and second. Tampa Bay has even used four outfielders (instead of the usual three) against some hitters. Teams are taking all the data that are out there and creating diagrams like spray charts to help their players. Teams see where a player is most likely to hit the ball, and they move players into those areas.

DEFENSIVE SHIFTS CAN MAKE FOR STRANGE ARRANGEMENTS, SUCH AS THESE FOUR PLAYERS POSITIONED BY THE DODGERS BETWEEN FIRST AND SECOND BASE.

SPRAY CHART

Check out this spray chart. For each of five main areas of the field, it shows how often (by percentage) Player A hit the ball. Higher percentages mean, naturally, more balls hit to those areas. Looking at these numbers, how would you shift your infielders to give them the best chance of catching a ball hit by this batter?

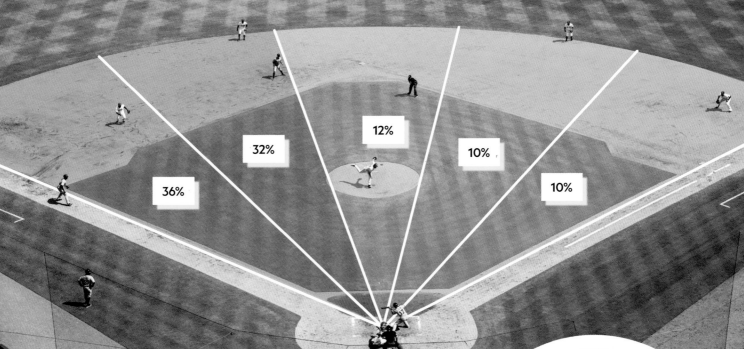

36% 32% 12% 10% 10%

RANGE FACTOR

Another way to measure defensive skill is with range factor. Range factor divides the total of putouts (PO) and assists (A) a player makes by the number of games (G) played. A higher number means a player made a lot of plays; that is, he had a lot of range, or covered a lot of ground on the field.

Here's the formula:

$$\frac{AP + PO}{G} = RF$$

The excellent Oakland third baseman Matt Chapman had 294 assists (A) and 139 putouts (PO) one season in which he played 145 games.

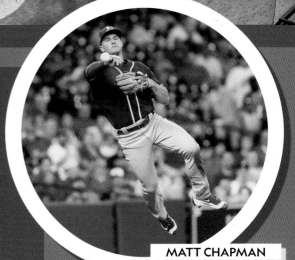

MATT CHAPMAN

$$\begin{array}{c} 294\ A \\ + \quad 139\ PO \\ \hline 433 \end{array} \quad \frac{433}{145} \rightarrow 145\ \sqrt{433} \quad \boxed{2.99\ RF}$$

PENCIL POWER

Which of these fielders' stats show the best RF?

DEREK JETER: 6,605 A, 3,820 PO, 2,674 G

CAL RIPKEN, JR.: 8,214 A, 4,112 PO, 2,977 G

ANSWER: Ripken's 4.14 beats Jeter's 3.90.

THE BALLPARK FACTOR

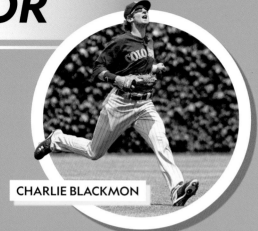

CHARLIE BLACKMON

The size of every ballpark's diamond is the same, but, as you know, every park is different. Outfields and locations affect game play. Some ballparks have natural grass, while a few use artificial turf. Some are covered, while others are open to the air. Some outfield fences are closer to home plate than in other parks. Colorado's Coors Field is a mile (1.6 km) above sea level where, at that altitude, the air is thinner. Thinner air affects how a ball carries when it's hit. Playing games in very hot or very cold weather can also affect the ball's flight.

The ballpark factor (BF) stat is used to compare all the MLB ballparks so that teams can see if a park favors hitters or pitchers. Lower ballpark factors favor pitchers because they mean fewer runs are scored. Higher ballpark factors mean there are a lot more runs, making them better places for hitters. Teams want to know all they can about their home ballpark, too, so they can choose players who will perform well there.

Here's the formula:

$$\frac{\text{Home } \frac{RS + RA}{G}}{\text{Road } \frac{RS + RA}{G}} = BF$$

home = at the home field   road = games played at the opponent's field
RS = runs scored   RA = runs allowed   G = games

In 2019, the Pittsburgh Pirates played in PNC Park. They played 81 games there and 81 games on the road. At home, they scored 342 runs and gave up 427. On the road, the Pittsburgh Pirates scored 375 runs and gave up 429.

HOME

$$\frac{342 + 427}{81} = \frac{769}{81} \rightarrow 81\sqrt{769} \; 9.49$$

ROAD

$$\frac{375 + 429}{81} = \frac{804}{81} \rightarrow 81\sqrt{804} \; 9.93$$

Home $\frac{9.49}{9.93}$ $\rightarrow$ $9.93\sqrt{9.49}$ **0.96 BF**

BRANDON WEBB

PENCIL POWER

Can you figure out the ballpark factor for Yankee Stadium using these sample stats?

411 homeRS	483 roadRS
303 homeRA	395 roadRA
81 homeG	81 roadG

ANSWER: .813 park factor for Yankee Stadium for those games

ORACLE PARK

PITCHER'S FAVORITE PARKS: LOWEST PARK FACTOR FOR RUNS

Oracle Park (San Francisco)	0.769
Petco Park (San Diego)	0.794
Yankee Stadium (New York City)	0.797
Wrigley Field (Chicago)	0.839
Target Field (Minneapolis)	0.850

HITTER'S HEAVENS: HIGHEST PARK FACTOR FOR RUNS

Coors Field (Denver)	1.611
Guaranteed Rate Field (Chicago)	1.148
PNC Park (Pittsburgh)	1.145
Oriole Park at Camden Yards (Baltimore)	1.142
SunTrust Park (near Atlanta)	1.123

STAT STORY

In thin air, a ball carries farther. To make playing in thin air as fair as playing at sea level, the folks at the Colorado Rockies came up with a solution. They keep the game balls in a special box called a humidor. This keeps the baseballs from drying out in Denver's thin, dry air. A ball that is dried out is lighter and thus will fly farther. In Colorado, add in the altitude—the ballpark is about a mile (1.6 km) above sea level so it has thinner air—and the thin air also lets baseballs fly farther. The Arizona Diamondbacks also use a humidor because the air in Phoenix is very dry. Keeping the balls from drying out is one way to make them similar in those cities to those in parks with more humidity. In fact, in 2018, MLB made every team store game balls the same way. After all, fair's fair!

INSIDE THE **BOX SCORE**

The box score is created once the game has ended. It packs all the information from a single baseball game into a tidy little stack of numbers and names. First widely used in the 1860s, the box score remains the best way to see nearly everything you need to know about a game in one glance. We've labeled a box score here so you can decipher it.

1. Line score
2. Winning pitcher
3. Losing pitcher
4. Batting lineup for each team
5. Player season averages calculated through the end of the game
6. Small letters show where pinch hitters came into the game
7. Extra-base hits
8. RISP: Runners in scoring position
9. Team fielding: Errors, double plays

HISTORY BY THE NUMBERS

Henry Chadwick invented the box score in 1859. Fans have been thanking him every day since. In just a few lines and using simple symbols, he came up with a way to sum up just about all the key things that happen in a baseball game. The box score has grown and evolved a little, but truthfully, it looks nearly the same as his first one. A key difference is that he included defensive stats and times that a batter was out because the game was much more defense-focused in those days. Today, there usually are no defensive stats in box scores.

STOLEN BASES

BASERUNNING

SB: Hamilton (18, 2nd base off Rodríguez/Vázquez); Dozier (2, 2nd base off Workman/Vázquez)

FIELDING

DP: 1 (Sparkman-O'Hearn)

PC-ST = PITCH COUNT AND STRIKES

Royals Pitching

PITCHERS	IP	H	R	ER	BB	K	HR	PC-ST	ERA
G. Sparkman	4.1	7	4	4	3	5	1	91-55	5.71
T. Hill	1	1	0	0	0	1	0	21-17	4.08
K. McCarthy	1	1	0	0	0	3	0	16-12	4.50
S. Barlow	0	0	0	0	1	1	0	18-11	5.60
J. Newberry	1.0	1	0	0	0	1	0	14-10	3.52
R. Lovelady (L, 0-3)	0.1	2	1	1	1	1	0	9-6	5.79
TEAM	9.1	12	5	5	5	12	1	169-111	

LIST OF PITCHERS FOR EACH TEAM, IN ORDER THEY APPEARED

PITCHING

IBB: Travis (by Lovelady).

First-pitch strikes/Batters Faced: Barlow 3/4; McCarthy 4/5; Sparkman 14/22; Newberry 2/4; Hill 5/5; Lovelady 2/4

Called strikes-Swinging strikes-Foul balls-In play strikes: Barlow-2-3-4-2; McCarthy-4-4-2-2; Sparkman-13-6-22-14; Newberry-2-1-4-3; Hill-5-1-7-3; Lovelady-2-1-1-2

Ground Balls-Fly Balls: Barlow 2-0; McCarthy 1-0; Sparkman 1-6; Newberry 1-1; Hill 2-1

Game Scores: G Sparkman 35

DETAILS OF SOME TYPES OF BALLS AND STRIKES

	1	2	3	4	5	6	7	8	9	10	R	H	E
KC	0	0	2	0	0	1	1	0	0	0	4	13	0
BOS	0	0	0	2	2	0	0	0	0	1	5	12	0

WIN
J. Taylor (1-1)
1.0 IP, 0 ER, 1 K, 0 BB

LOSS
R. Lovelady (0-2)
0.1 IP, 1 ER, 1 K, 1 BB

Royals Hitting

HITTERS	AB	R	H	RBI	BB	K	AVG	OBP	SLG
W. Merrifield LF	5	0	2	1	0	0	.302	.357	.477
H. Arteaga SS	5	0	1	0	0	1	.190	.238	.215
H. Dozier RF	5	1	2	0	0	1	.282	.367	.526
J. Soler DH	4	1	1	0	1	2	.253	.335	.527
C. Cuthbert 3B	3	1	1	0	2	0	.290	.329	.434
N. Lopez 2B	5	0	2	1	0	1	.224	.265	.290
M. Viloria C	4	0	2	2	0	2	.263	.333	.395
a - N. Dini PH-C	1	0	0	0	0	0	.000	.000	.000
R. O'Hearn 1B	5	0	0	0	0	3	.171	.265	.310
B. Hamilton CF	4	1	2	0	0	1	.213	.279	.270
b - B. Starling PH-CF	1	0	0	0	0	0	.234	.263	.338
TEAM	**42**	**4**	**13**	**4**	**3**	**10**			

Red Sox Hitting

HITTERS	AB	R	H	RBI	BB	K	AVG	OBP	SLG
M. Betts RF	4	1	2	0	1	1	.282	.390	.487
R. Devers 3B	4	1	0	0	1	3	.318	.367	.563
X. Bogaerts SS	5	1	3	2	0	0	.310	.389	.566
J.D. Martinez DH	5	1	2	2	0	1	.302	.377	.546
A. Benintendi LF	5	0	1	0	0	3	.284	.355	.467
C. Vazquez C	5	0	1	0	0	0	.283	.322	.490
C. Owings PR	0	1	0	0	0	0	.133	.193	.222
M. Moreland 1B	4	0	1	0	0	1	.222	.304	.494
a - S. Travis PH	0	0	0	0	1	0	.250	.294	.400
B. Holt 2B	3	0	2	1	2	0	.318	.385	.405
J. Bradley Jr. CF	4	0	0	0	0	3	.219	.313	.386
TEAM	**39**	**5**	**12**	**5**	**5**	**12**			

a-lined out to first for Viloria in the 10th
b-grounded to shortstop for Hamilton in the 10th

BATTING
2B: Hamilton (12, D. Hernandez); N. Lopez (15, Eovaldi)
RBI: Merrifield (65), N. Lopez (20), Viloria 2 (9)
2Out RBI: Merrifield, N. Lopez, Viloria (2)
Team RISP: 4-11 (Cuthbert 0-2, Merrifield 1-2, O'Hearn 0-1, N. Lopez 2-4, Viloria 1-2)
Team LOB: 11

BASERUNNING
SB: Hamilton (18, 2nd base off Rodríguez/Vázquez); Dozier (2, 2nd base off Workman/Vázquez)

FIELDING
DP: 1 (Sparkman-O'Hearn)

a-intentionally walked for Moreland in the 10th

BATTING
2B: Vázquez (22, Lovelady); Bogaerts (43, Sparkman)
HR: Martinez (28, 4th inning off Sparkman 1 on, 0 Out)
RBI: Holt (23), Martinez 2 (75), Bogaerts 2 (94)
Team RISP: 3-5 (Holt 1-1, Martinez 1-1, Vázquez 0-1, Bogaerts 1-1, Benintendi 0-1)
Team LOB: 11

FIELDING
DP: 1 (Bradley Jr.-Devers)
Assists: Bradley Jr. (Hamilton at 3rd base)

Royals Pitching

PITCHERS	IP	H	R	ER	BB	K	HR	PC-ST	ERA
G. Sparkman	4.1	7	4	4	4	5	1	91-55	5.71
T. Hill	1.1	1	0	0	0	1	0	21-17	4.08
K. McCarthy	1.1	1	0	0	0	3	0	16-12	4.50
S. Barlow	1.0	0	0	0	1	1	0	18-11	5.60
J. Newberry	1.0	1	0	0	0	1	0	14-10	3.52
R. Lovelady (L, 0-3)	0.1	2	1	1	1	1	0	9-6	5.79
TEAM	**9.1**	**12**	**5**	**5**	**5**	**12**	**1**	**169-111**	

PITCHING
IBB: Travis (by Lovelady).
First-pitch strikes/Batters Faced: Barlow 3/4; McCarthy 4/5; Sparkman 14/22; Newberry 2/4; Hill 5/5; Lovelady 2/4
Called strikes-Swinging strikes-Foul balls-In play strikes: Barlow-2-3-4-2; McCarthy-4-4-2-2; Sparkman-13-6-22-14; Newberry-2-1-4-3; Hill-5-1-7-3; Lovelady-2-1-1-2
Ground Balls-Fly Balls: Barlow 2-0; McCarthy 1-0; Sparkman 1-6; Newberry 1-1; Hill 2-1
Game Scores: G Sparkman 35

Red Sox Pitching

PITCHERS	IP	H	R	ER	BB	K	HR	PC-ST	ERA
E. Rodriguez	5.0	7	2	2	3	1	0	101-60	4.17
D. Hernandez (H, 2)	1.0	2	1	1	0	2	0	15-10	2.35
N. Eovaldi (B, 1)	2.0	3	1	1	0	5	0	36-28	6.59
B. Workman	1.0	1	0	0	0	1	0	15-9	1.95
J. Taylor (W, 1-1)	1.0	0	0	0	0	1	0	13-7	3.60
TEAM	**10.0**	**13**	**4**	**4**	**3**	**10**	**0**	**180-114**	

PITCHING
WP: Eovaldi
First-pitch strikes/Batters Faced: Eovaldi 6/9; Rodríguez 16/24; Workman 1/4; Taylor 0/3; D. Hernandez 1/5
Called strikes-Swinging strikes-Foul balls-In play strikes: Eovaldi-10-7-7-4; Rodríguez-13-11-16-19; Workman-4-2-0-3; Taylor-4-0-1-2; D. Hernandez-3-3-1-3
Ground Balls-Fly Balls: Eovaldi 1-0; Rodríguez 6-7; Workman 1-1; Taylor 1-1; D. Hernandez 0-1
Game Scores: E Rodriguez 43

TRY *THIS!*

What's Your Personal Spray Chart?

On page 88, you read about spray charts. Now it's time to make one of your own. Instead of charting where you hit a baseball most often, your spray chart will show you where you hang out most often during a given week.

WHAT YOU NEED:

- Paper
- A pen

1 On your paper, write out a weekly calendar.

2 On Monday, list in order all the places you go. Bedroom, bathroom, kitchen, backyard, car, school, bus, gym, and so on.

3 As the week goes on, make a tally mark each time you visit one of these places again. Add new places as they come up (practice field, music class, restaurant, etc.).

4 On Sunday night, before bed, add up all your tallies. For example, how many times total during the week did you go to the bathroom?

5 Using the map or bar graph described below, draw your spray chart.

WEEKLY PLAN OF ACTION

monday
my room ||||
kitchen ||||
bathroom ||||
school |

baseball
practice |

backyard |

tuesday
my room ||||
kitchen ||||
bathroom ||||
school |

friend's house |

wednesday
my room ||||
kitchen ||||||
bathroom ||||
school |

baseball
practice |

backyard |

thursday
my room |||
kitchen ||||||
bathroom ||||
school |

backyard |

friday
my room ||||||
kitchen ||||
bathroom ||||||
school |

friend's house |

saturday
baseball game |

sunday
friend's house |

notes

TOTALS
bathroom = 24   backyard = 3
my room = 22   school = 5
kitchen = 30   baseball
friend's house = 3
practice = 2   baseball game = 1

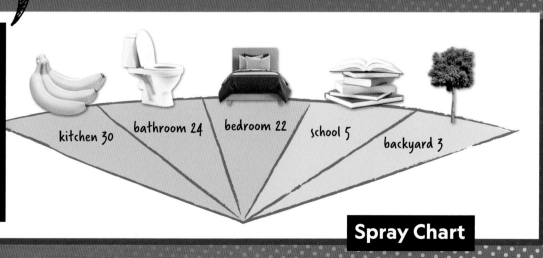

My room 22 · bath 24 · kitchen 30 · backyard 3 · school 5 · friend's house 3 · baseball practice 2

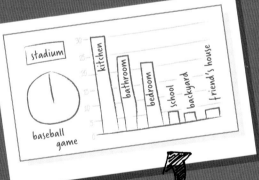

stadium

kitchen · bathroom · bedroom · school · backyard · friend's house

baseball game

Map
Draw your neighborhood or your town, including all the places you visited. You can then use a color code to fill in each place: Perhaps red is the "hottest," since you went there most often. Or you can just use the total of tallies, such as 11 for the kitchen or whatever number you came up with.

Bar Graph
Start by adding up the tallies. Then draw a bar graph with the location most visited as the tallest bar. Make each of the other bars smaller, based on the total for each location.

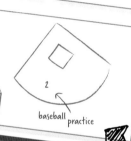

kitchen 30   bathroom 24   bedroom 22   school 5   backyard 3

Spray Chart

CHAPTER SIX

THE WORLD (SERIES)

OF BASEBALL

After the regular season, the top teams of the American League and the National League battle in three rounds of playoffs before they meet in the World Series. The winner of the World Series is the season champion. Calling it the *World* Series doesn't actually describe who plays, considering that until 1969, when the Canadian Montreal Expos joined MLB, only teams playing in U.S. cities were on the field. Today it is still true that only North American teams compete. Not exactly the whole world.

Of course, baseball is played in many countries. It has even been part of the Olympics. The World Baseball Classic has matched about 20 teams from various nations against each other since 2006. Youth baseball is also played around the world, and the Little League World Series is a huge annual event. And don't forget baseball's Midsummer Classic, the awesome All-Star Game, and even women's pro baseball. In this chapter, we'll look at the numbers for baseball's biggest days and its future superstars.

HISTORY BY THE NUMBERS

Through 2019, the World Series has been played every year since 1903 … with two exceptions:

1904: A year after the first World Series, the NL champion New York Giants refused to play the AL champion Boston Red Sox. Giants manager John McGraw did not consider the AL—then only three years old—worthy of playing his team. (The NL had begun in 1876.)

1994: Players and owners argued about the way that players were paid. After negotiations fell apart, the owners stopped paying and the players stopped playing. The season ended in August without a World Series being played.

MLB **PLAYOFFS** BY THE **NUMBERS**

From 1903 to 1968, the World Series teams were easy to spot: You needed only to look at the top of the final standings for the AL and NL. In 1969, MLB added a new level of competition. Because the number of teams in the league had grown in the 1960s, the AL and NL were split into two divisions each. The League Championship Series (LCS) was created to match the winners of the two divisions in each league. The LCS champs then met in the World Series. In 1995, with baseball having grown to 30 teams and three divisions per league, another round was added—the Division Series. Each of the division champs was joined by a fourth "wild card" team. This was the second-place team with the best record. Since 2012, two wild card teams in each league have faced off in a one-game playoff to see who can play in the Division Series. Whew!

MLB PLAYOFFS

AL DIVISION SERIES

ALCS

AL WILD-CARD PLAYOFF

WORLD SERIES

VS

NL DIVISION SERIES

NLCS

NL WILD-CARD PLAYOFF

POSTSEASON KINGS

Check out these records set during the playoffs since 1969. Players since 1995 dominate the rankings because they have had at least one extra round in which to pile up stats.

Most At Bats:	Derek Jeter, 650
Most Homers:	Manny Ramirez, 29
Most RBIs:	Bernie Williams, 80
Highest BA:	Bobby Brown, .439
Most SBs:	Kenny Lofton, 34
Best ERA:	Mariano Rivera, 0.70
Most Wins:	Andy Pettitte, 19
Most Saves:	Mariano Rivera, 42
Most Strikeouts:	Justin Verlander, 202

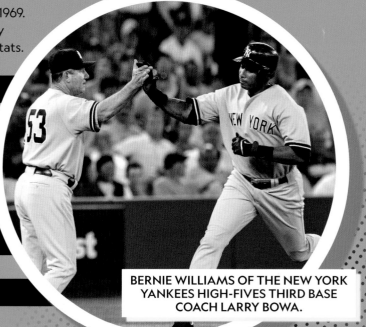

BERNIE WILLIAMS OF THE NEW YORK YANKEES HIGH-FIVES THIRD BASE COACH LARRY BOWA.

TAMPA BAY RAYS

MAGIC NUMBERS

Baseball has "magic numbers"! These are the sum of two things: the amount of wins still needed by a team in first place, plus the amount of losses they need the second place team to get, in order to clinch a division title. Win a game, and your magic number goes down. If your opponent loses, the number goes down again. Many websites and newspapers post the magic number in the standings. When the magic number reaches zero, the team in first has won.

Look at these sample standings:

NL WEST	W–L
Los Angeles Dodgers	98–52
Arizona Diamondbacks	89–61
San Francisco Giants	75–75
San Diego Padres	74–76
Colorado Rockies	69–81

Here's the formula:

(162 Games in a Season + 1) – Wins So Far – Losses by Second Place Team = Magic number

162 games + 1 – 98 Dodger wins so far – 61 Diamondbacks losses → 162 + 1 – 98 – 61 = 4 the magic number

$$+\ \begin{array}{r} 162 \text{ games} \\ 1 \\ \hline 163 \end{array} \qquad -\ \begin{array}{r} 163 \\ 98 \text{ wins so far} \\ \hline 65 \end{array} \qquad -\ \begin{array}{r} 65 \\ 61 \text{ losses} \\ \hline 4 \text{ Magic Number} \end{array}$$

With 12 games left in the 162-game season, any combination of Dodgers wins and Diamondbacks losses that totals four means LA clinches the division title.

PENCIL POWER

Given these stats, what was the Houston Astros' magic number against the second-place team Oakland A's?

Houston 100–51   Oakland 93–58

ANSWER: 5

99

WORLD SERIES **WINNERS**

From the first day of spring training, the goal of every MLB team is to make it to the World Series, aka the Fall Classic. Every player wants to lift the Commissioner's Trophy and get those coveted World Series rings. Each season, though, only one team is able to enjoy all of that. Here's a numbers-packed look at the best of the best of the best.

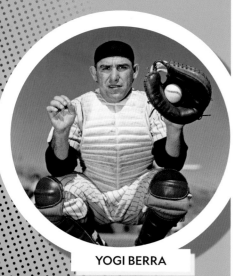

SANDY KOUFAX

MOST WORLD SERIES CHAMPIONSHIPS BY TEAM
(Last title year in parentheses.)

27	New York Yankees (2009)
11	St. Louis Cardinals (2011)
9	Boston Red Sox (2018)
9	Philadelphia/Oakland Athletics (1989)
8	New York/San Francisco Giants (2014)
6	Brooklyn/Los Angeles Dodgers (1988)
5	Pittsburgh Pirates (1979)
5	Cincinnati Reds (1990)

WORLD SERIES MVP AWARDS

First given in 1955, the MVP award is voted on by the Baseball Writers Association of America and is given during the postgame ceremonies. Since 2017, the World Series MVP award has been named in honor of San Francisco/New York Giants superstar Willie Mays. Only pitchers Sandy Koufax (1963 and 1965), Bob Gibson (1964 and 1967), and outfielder Reggie "Mr. October" Jackson (1973 and 1977) have won the award more than once. Here's a list of the positions that World Series MVP winners have played.

P	29
3B	10
OF	9
C	7
SS	5
DH	3
1B	3
2B	1

MOST WORLD SERIES CHAMPIONSHIPS BY PLAYER

Believe it or not, ALL except one of these men won all their World Series rings with the New York Yankees. (Babe Ruth won seven rings, but only four with the Yankees; three were with the Boston Red Sox).

10	Yogi Berra
9	Joe DiMaggio
7	Bill Dickey
	Phil Rizzuto
	Hank Bauer
	Mickey Mantle
	Babe Ruth

YOGI BERRA

WASHINGTON NATIONALS CELEBRATE BEATING THE HOUSTON ASTROS 6–2 IN GAME 7 OF THE WORLD SERIES AT MINUTE MAID PARK ON WEDNESDAY, OCTOBER 30, 2019.

DIGIT-YOU-KNOW?

The World Series is a best-of-seven contest. The first team to win four games is the champ. From 1919 to 1921, however, MLB experimented with a best-of-nine format. The winners had to capture five games instead of four.

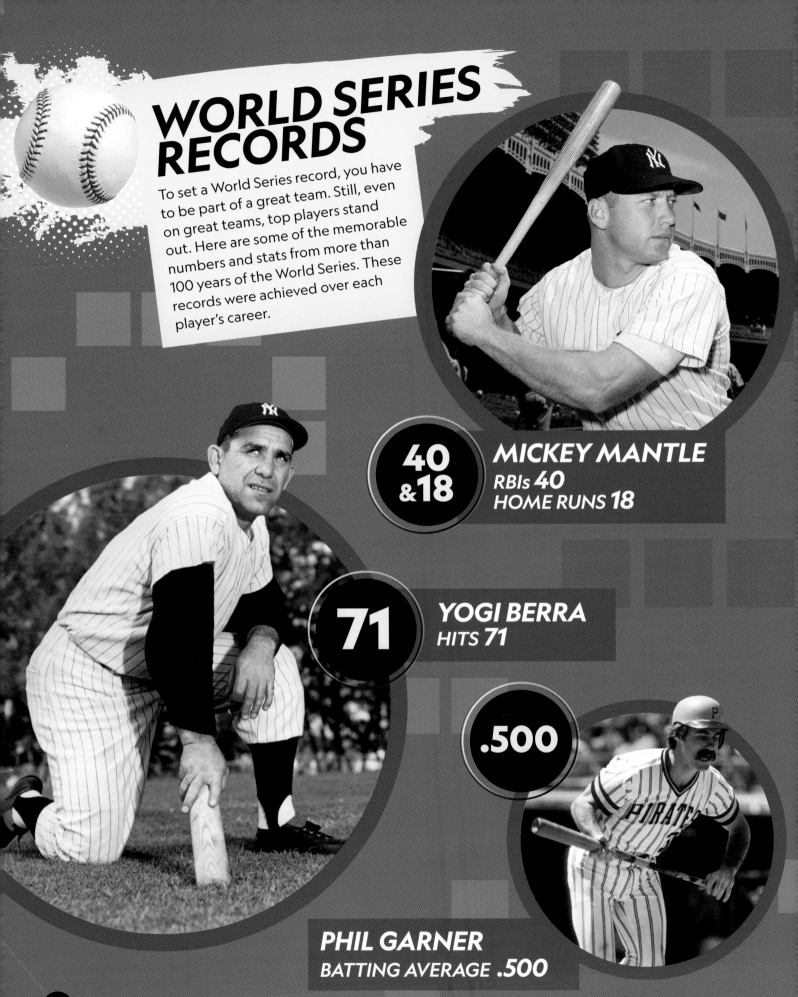

WORLD SERIES RECORDS

To set a World Series record, you have to be part of a great team. Still, even on great teams, top players stand out. Here are some of the memorable numbers and stats from more than 100 years of the World Series. These records were achieved over each player's career.

40 & 18

MICKEY MANTLE
RBIs **40**
HOME RUNS **18**

71

YOGI BERRA
HITS **71**

.500

PHIL GARNER
BATTING AVERAGE **.500**

MADISON BUMGARNER
ERA **0.25** (AS OF 2019)

0.25

10
&**94**

WHITEY FORD
WINS **10**
STRIKEOUTS **94**

11

MARIANO RIVERA
SAVES **11**

YOGI BERRA AND
DON LARSEN (R)

HISTORY BY THE NUMBERS
A perfect game is when a pitcher does not allow a single opponent to reach a base by any means. The only perfect game in World Series history came in Game 2, 1956. Don Larsen of the Yankees pitched to beat the Brooklyn Dodgers 2–0. Larsen was as surprised as the fans that he pitched a perfect game; he didn't even know he was the starting pitcher until he got to the ballpark!

BEYOND THE **WORLD SERIES**

Ever since 1933, the best players from the AL and NL have been selected to play in the MLB All-Star Game, also called the Midsummer Classic. Until 2019, the only year the game was not played was 1945, due to World War II. In most seasons, fans help choose the teams by voting who they consider the best players. Team managers and MLB staff make other selections. At least one player from every team is chosen to play.

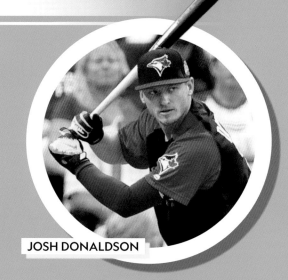

JOSH DONALDSON

JOSH HAMILTON

MOST VOTES BY FANS

These players all set the record for most votes, back when fans could vote as often as they wanted! But the way that fans vote has changed over the years.

14,090,188	Josh Donaldson, 3B, Toronto Blue Jays, 2015
11,073,744	Josh Hamilton, OF, Texas Rangers, 2012
8,272,243	Chris Davis, 1B, Baltimore Orioles, 2013
7,454,753	Jose Bautista, 3B, Toronto Blue Jays, 2011
6,079,688	Ken Griffey, Jr., OF, Seattle Mariners, 1994

ALL-STAR GAME ALL-TIME RECORD

The All-Star Game (ASG) pits one league against the other. Most fans cheer for the league in which their favorite team plays. The two leagues have been pretty evenly matched over the years. As of 2019, the AL has won 45 All-Star Games, while the NL has won 43! (Two games ended in ties—in 1961 and 2002.) Each league has had an impressive winning streak in the ASG, though. The AL won 13 games in a row from 1997 through 2009. From 1972 through 1982, the NL reeled off 11 straight wins.

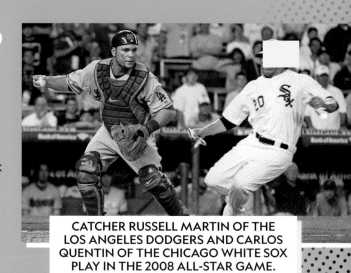

CATCHER RUSSELL MARTIN OF THE LOS ANGELES DODGERS AND CARLOS QUENTIN OF THE CHICAGO WHITE SOX PLAY IN THE 2008 ALL-STAR GAME.

EDDIE STUMPF AND
THE ROCKFORD PEACHES
OF THE ALL-AMERICAN
GIRLS PROFESSIONAL
BASEBALL LEAGUE

THE WOMEN'S CHAMPS

The All-American Girls Professional Baseball
League, active from 1943–54 (page 21), held
an annual championship as well, but they
didn't call it the World Series. The top two
teams met at the end of each season. With
four titles, the Rockford Peaches were the
New York Yankees of the AAGPBL.

1943	Racine Belles
1944	Milwaukee Chicks
1945	Rockford Peaches
1946	Racine Belles
1947	Grand Rapids Chicks
1948	Rockford Peaches
1949	Rockford Peaches
1950	Rockford Peaches
1951	South Bend Blue Sox
1952	South Bend Blue Sox
1953	Grand Rapids Chicks
1954	Kalamazoo Lassies

INTERNATIONAL **BASEBALL**

Baseball was born in the United States, but many of its earliest players had grown up playing cricket, a bat-and-ball game popular in England. Americans helped spread the game when they traveled the world. A professor named Horace Wilson introduced the sport to Japan in the late 1860s. American military personnel brought the game to places such as Cuba in the late 1800s. In recent decades, countries such as Australia, South Korea, and the Netherlands have also seen baseball played at a professional level. Today, 141 countries are members of the World Baseball Softball Confederation.

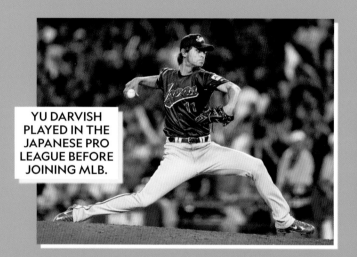

YU DARVISH PLAYED IN THE JAPANESE PRO LEAGUE BEFORE JOINING MLB.

JAPANESE CHAMPIONS

Next to MLB, the Japanese pro league is the oldest in the world, playing its first season in 1936. These teams have won the most championships in what is now called the Nippon Baseball League.

TITLES	TEAM
22	Yomiuri Giants
13	Saitama Seibu Lions
9	Fukuoka SoftBank Hawks
5	Tokyo Yakult Swallows

BASEBALL IN THE OLYMPICS

Baseball was a "demonstration" sport at six Olympics, starting in 1912. This means that nations are allowed to choose such sports to add to their Olympic lineup. The winners do not get official Olympic medals. In 1992, it became an official medal sport. Unfortunately, it was voted out of the lineup after the 2008 Games, but efforts continue to bring it back in future Olympics.

SOUTH KOREAN PLAYERS TOSS MANAGER KIM KYUNG-MOON AS THEY CELEBRATE THEIR VICTORY OVER CUBA AT THE 2008 BEIJING OLYMPIC GAMES.

EDUARDO PARET OF CUBA WITH WILLY TAVERAS OF THE DOMINICAN REPUBLIC AT THE WBC

INTERNATIONAL MLB PLAYERS

Each year, MLB teams include lots of players who were born outside the United States. They come from many places, but most often from Central and South America. These are the places that sent the most players to MLB in 2019.

PLAYERS	NATION
102	Dominican Republic
68	Venezuela
19	Cuba
18	Puerto Rico
8	Mexico
6	Japan
6	Canada

The following countries sent one player each to MLB in 2019: Aruba, Australia, Brazil, Germany, Lithuania, Netherlands, Nicaragua, Panama, Taiwan, and the U.S. Virgin Islands.

WORLD BASEBALL CLASSIC

In 2006, Major League Baseball worked with international baseball officials to create the first World Baseball Classic. Nations were invited to put together teams of players from their countries. Some MLB players played for their home countries' teams. Many players found themselves facing their regular season MLB teammates on opposing teams.

2017	United States 8, Puerto Rico 0
2013	Dominican Republic 3, Puerto Rico 0
2009	Japan 5, South Korea 3
2006	Japan 10, Cuba 6

* Even though Puerto Rico and the U.S. Virgin Islands are U.S. territories, MLB classifies them as separate countries.

RISING **STARS**

Just about every big-league star started out playing in some sort of youth baseball league or team. The biggest youth baseball organization in the world is Little League Baseball, which was founded in Williamsport, Pennsylvania, in 1939. It includes baseball and softball programs for kids ages 4–16 and culminates each year with the Little League World Series (LLWS) for the 10–12-year-old division. The final game of the LLWS pits the champion of the international division against the top U.S. team.

COLLEGE

College baseball has its own World Series. Held each summer in Omaha, Nebraska, the College World Series (CWS) matches the best Division I teams in the National Collegiate Athletic Association (NCAA). Eight teams make the final tournament, with the winner determined after a final best-of-three playoff. These schools have won the most CWS championships:

**KEVIN GINKEL
ARIZONA WILDCATS**

CWS TITLES	SCHOOL (YEAR LAST WON)
12	University of Southern California (1998)
6	Louisiana State University (2009)
6	University of Texas (2005)
5	Arizona State University (1981)
4	University of Arizona (2012)
4	Cal State Fullerton (2004)
4	University of Miami (2001)

LLWS WINNERS

These countries have captured the most Little League World Series championships. Mexico was the first country outside the United States to win, in 1957. Teams from Taiwan dominated in the 1970s and 1980s.

TITLES	COUNTRY
36	United States
17	Taiwan
11	Japan
3	Mexico
3	South Korea

LITTLE LEAGUE PLAYERS FROM REYNOSA, MEXICO, CELEBRATE A LLWS SEMI-FINAL VICTORY IN 2009.

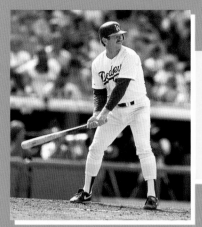

HISTORY BY THE NUMBERS

A handful of players have played in both the LLWS and the MLB World Series. Rick Dempsey was a winner in both! His LL team from California won it all in 1963. Twenty years later, Dempsey was a catcher and the World Series MVP on the 1983 Baltimore Orioles. He won again while playing with the 1988 Los Angeles Dodgers.

STAT STORY

Girls were finally allowed to play Little League Baseball in 1974. Through 2019, 19 girls were on teams that made it all the way to the Little League World Series. In 2014, Mo'ne Davis made world headlines when, as the only girl on her Atlanta team, she led them to the LLWS, and had a 70-mile-an-hour (113-km/h) pitch at only 13 years old. A fireballing right-hander, she pitched a shutout in the tournament and was named the SI Kids SportsKid of the Year. Davis was the first African-American girl to play in the LLWS. She later showed us she wasn't just amazing at baseball. She went on to also become a top basketball player in high school, and then played college athletics.

TRY *THIS!*

500

How do you play or practice baseball if you only have a few people ... and no baseball diamond? Easy. You play 500! This is an old, traditional baseball practice game that is also really fun to play.

WHAT YOU NEED:

- Some sort of field or playground
- A ball of some kind: Tennis balls work great, but you can play with a baseball if everyone has gloves.
- A bat, though you can also throw the ball instead of hitting it. It's up to you.
- Pencil and paper to keep score, or you can try to do that in your head.

1 One person is chosen as the batter (or thrower). The rest of the players stand out in the field. How far? Depends how far the batter or thrower can send the ball!

**Fly Ball
100 Points**

2 The batter tosses the ball up and hits it toward the players in the field. They all try to catch it.

Who caught it? The person who did gets points like this:
- **Fly ball: 100 points**
- **Line drive: 75 points**
- **Ground ball: 25 points**

Did a fielder make an error? That is, did they try to grab the ball and miss or have it bounce off their hands? That's minus 100 points!

Keep track of everyone's points as you go.

**Line Drive
75 Points**

**Ground Ball
25 Points**

The first person to reach or go over 500 total points wins.

CHAPTER SEVEN

9 CRAZY

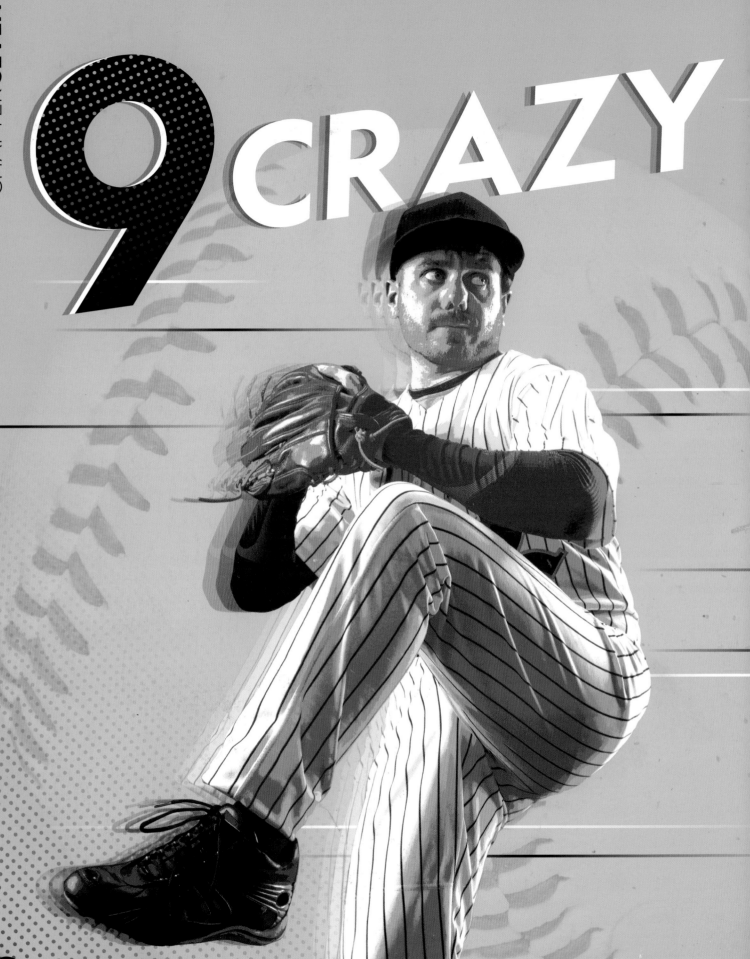

NUMBERS

Nine is a magic number in baseball. Nine innings. Nine players on the field. Nine players in the batting order. In baseball, as in many sports, some numbers instantly mean more than just a stat or a year. Here's an introduction to nine famous numbers. Can you find even more magic baseball numbers?

DIGIT-YOU-KNOW?

In 2016, a set of documents came to light that solidified baseball history. The "Laws of Base Ball" were written in 1857 by Daniel Lucius "Doc" Adams, a member of the famous Knickerbocker Baseball Club. It was the first time that the rules were written down and agreed to by all clubs. Before that year, amateur clubs that played "base ball" throughout the Northeast played by a variety of rules. Some played until 21 runs instead of nine innings. Some had 10 fielders. At the 1857 meeting, the clubs agreed to nine players and nine innings. And it's been that way ever since!

42

Brooklyn Dodgers general manager Branch Rickey did not agree with baseball's racist ban of African-American players. He wanted to change it, so he sought to find a talented player who could help change hearts and minds. Jackie Robinson had grown up in Pasadena, California. He and his brother Mack were great athletes (Mack ran in the Olympics). Jackie Robinson went to UCLA, where he was a star on many sport teams. He also was an officer in the U.S. Army during World War II, before joining the Kansas City Monarchs, a charter member of the Negro National League. After signing with the Dodgers in 1945, Robinson played a year in the minors in Montreal. Then, on April 15, 1947, he debuted in MLB, wearing No. 42 for the Brooklyn Dodgers. In the face of near constant threats, insults, and danger, Robinson broke records and created an enduring legacy. He was the 1947 Rookie of the Year, after leading the NL in stolen bases—and the 1949 MVP, when he led the league with a .342 batting average. In 1955, he helped the Dodgers win the World Series.

HISTORY BY THE NUMBERS

Robinson's No. 42 was retired by every MLB team in 1997. In 1987, Robinson had received another honor. That year, MLB renamed the annual Rookie of the Year Award for him. Baseball writers choose the best first-year player from each league. Many former Rookies of the Year have gone on to Hall of Fame careers, so keep an eye on these players.

56

Getting a hit in one game is pretty routine. Getting hits a few games in a row has happened to most players. But the more games you play, the harder it is to get a hit in each and every one. That's why Joe DiMaggio's 56-game hitting streak in 1941 remains one of baseball's iconic records. "Joltin' Joe" was an all-around star for the New York Yankees. He joined the team in 1936 and helped them win four straight World Series. Then in 1941, he thrilled fans and teammates by getting at least one hit in 56 games in a row. He ended up winning the batting title and another World Series ring. After missing three years of baseball while serving in World War II, DiMaggio returned and helped the Yanks win four more championships. The list below shows who came closest (in one season) to the incredible 56 in a row by the "Yankee Clipper."

LONGEST HITTING STREAKS

56	Joe DiMaggio, 1941
44	Willie Keeler, 1896–97
44	Pete Rose, 1978
42	Bill Dahlen, 1984
41	George Sisler, 1922
40	Ty Cobb, 1911
39	Paul Molitor, 1987

86 AND 108*

DAVID ORTIZ

A few years ago, these numbers were VERY familiar to fans of two teams. First, the Boston Red Sox: The Sox won the World Series in 1918 and then waited 86 years until they won another, in 2004. They came close a few times, reaching the Series four times but never getting a win. When they won in '04, it broke the "Curse of the Bambino." Boston slugger Babe "The Bambino" Ruth left for the Yankees in 1920 and after that, the Red Sox didn't win for another 84 years. Some fans blamed the curse on the terrible deal that let Ruth go.

In Chicago, they had another curse. The Cubs won the 1908 World Series. They didn't make the Fall Classic again until 1945. There, a fan tried to bring a lucky goat into a game. The Cubs said no, so the owner put the "Billy Goat Curse" on the team. The Cubs didn't make the World Series again until 2016. That put their no-trophy streak at 108 years. However, in 2016, the curse was lifted. The Cubs beat the Cleveland Indians in seven thrilling games to finally bring the championship to Wrigley Field.

*Okay, sure, we have two numbers here. But they are part of the ONE story about waiting a long time for success!

STILL WAITING

These Major League teams have never won a World Series.

TEAM	FIRST MLB SEASON
Texas Rangers	1961
Milwaukee Brewers	1969
San Diego Padres	1969
Seattle Mariners	1977
Colorado Rockies	1993
Tampa Bay Rays	1998

THE CHICAGO CUBS CELEBRATE AFTER WINNING GAME SEVEN OF THE 2016 WORLD SERIES.

511

Of all the baseball records, this is one of the most unbreakable. Denton True "Cy" Young piled up 511 pitching victories in his amazing career. No one will ever approach that. Baseball today is much different than when Young pitched. During 12 different seasons, he started in 35 or more games. Only a handful of pitchers reach 35 starts a season these days.

How far are today's pitchers from Young's 511? In 2019, CC Sabathia of the New York Yankees retired. He had the most career wins of any pitcher who was active in 2019. Sabathia's total (which is still impressive) was 251. That's not even half of what Young did! Cy's record is safe.

CHASING YOUNG

Young is far ahead of even these great pitching heroes.

PLAYER (YEARS PLAYED), CAREER WINS
Walter Johnson (1907–27), 417
Pete Alexander (1911–30), 373
Christy Mathewson (1900–16), 373
Warren Spahn (1942–65), 363

HISTORY BY THE NUMBERS

How did Young get his nickname? Many people thought it was because he threw like a cyclone, a powerful storm with high winds. In fact, the nickname "Cyrus" was common in the late 1800s for a person from a rural background. Because Young grew up on a farm in Ohio, his urban, big-league teammates teased him by calling him Cyrus or Cy.

CY YOUNG

714

Only two players have topped Babe Ruth's incredible record of 714 homers. But no one can top the Bambino's epic life and his impact on the sport. He helped change baseball from a game of small hits, bunts, and running into one of big blasts, long balls, and power. Before he came along, a batter might lead his league with fewer than 10 homers. Ruth set a new single-season record with 29 homers in 1919, and then broke it himself three times! He was the first ever to reach 30, 40, 50, and 60 homers in a season. When he hit 54 in 1920, that was more than each of the other seven American League teams. His power hitting and his outsize personality made him the first national sports super-star. His career slugging average of .690 remains the best of all time, more than 84 seasons since he retired!

BOLD BABE

On baseball websites or on the back of baseball cards, if a player leads a league in a stat category, the number for that stat appears in bold type. Few players can match the bold type of the Babe.

STAT	NUMBER OF YEARS BABE LED AL
Slugging Average	13
On-Base Percentage	10
Home Runs	12
Walks	11
Runs	8
Total Bases	6
RBIs	5

1919

To a baseball fan, some years stand out in history more than others, and 1919 means one thing: the Black Sox Scandal. In the first decades of Major League Baseball, players were not paid the enormous sums seen today. Most had jobs in the offseason. When players were given the chance to make more money, they sometimes took it. However, when some players took money from gamblers to "throw" a game, or lose on purpose, they crossed the line, doing something illegal and immoral. Members of the AL Champion Chicago White Sox were paid to lose some games to the Cincinnati Reds. Knowing how the game would end, gamblers could make bets against the Sox that were guaranteed to pay them big money.

The underdog Reds were the surprise winners of the Series. But by the following spring, an investigation led to the White Sox players being caught. They became known as the "Black Sox." Though they were not convicted of an actual crime in court, the incident left a stain on the game. The players were kicked off their team and banned from playing professionally.

HISTORY BY THE NUMBERS

One of the players accused in the scandal was also one of the greatest hitters in baseball history. "Shoeless" Joe Jackson's .356 lifetime average is still the third-best ever. He apparently never took money, and he played his best in the Series. But he knew of the gamblers' bribes and didn't tell. In the years since, many have felt sorry for Jackson. Some people think he should be forgiven and let into the Hall of Fame. Others think he should stay out. What do you think?

THE CHICAGO WHITE SOX, 1919

.406

In 1941, the batting average of the great Ted Williams was .406. He was the last player to top .400 for a season. No one has come closer than .390 since then. When Williams was growing up in San Diego, he was obsessed with hitting. He famously said that when he was a kid, he told people, "When I walk down the street, I want everyone to say, 'There goes the greatest hitter who ever lived.'" He pretty much made that come true. He joined the Boston Red Sox in 1939 and set the MLB rookie record with 145 RBIs. Two years later, he charged through the season toward the magic .400 mark. On the final day of the season, his batting average was .3995. If he didn't play, it would be rounded up to .400. But that was not how "Teddy Ballgame" played. If he played and did not get any hits, his average would have fallen below .400. It was a big risk. But he played, got six hits in eight at bats, and ended up at .406. He later missed most of five seasons when he served as a pilot in the U.S. military, but he still ended up with a career average of .344 and 521 homers. He led the AL in hitting six times and in walks eight times, and his .482 OBP is still the best ever.

TED WILLIAMS

3,000

The ultimate goal for MLB hitters is to join the exclusive 3,000-Hit Club. Piling up that many hits takes years and years of hard work and effort, and a little luck. Through 2019, only 32 players have gotten at least 3,000 hits. Pete Rose (1963–86) leads the pack with 4,256. The only other player to top 4,000 hits was Ty Cobb (1905–28), a Detroit Tigers legend who played 24 seasons. As of the end of the 2019 season, only two current players were within 500 hits of joining this exclusive club!

PETE ROSE

2,632

Baseball is a grind. Players are on the field nearly every day for about six months. Today's players also have to spend many hours on airplanes flying around the country (and now, sometimes, around the world) for games. They can be injured, they can get sick, and they are replaced by others. So, when you see a player who can string together a streak of playing in 2,632 straight games, that is something really, really special. In 1995, Baltimore Orioles infielder Cal Ripken, Jr., topped the consecutive-games record of the great Lou Gehrig, who played 2,130 in a row. Ripken kept the streak going until 1998. Finally, that September he said, "It was time." He wanted to end it in front of his loyal Orioles fans. This is a record that will surely never be topped.

CAL RIPKEN, JR.

HISTORY BY THE NUMBERS

The Ripkens were a real baseball family. Cal Ripken, Sr., was a longtime minor-league coach and also managed the Orioles from 1985 to 1988. Cal Ripken, Jr., was a Hall of Fame shortstop. Cal Jr.'s brother Billy had a 12-year MLB career and is now a popular TV announcer. They're not alone. More than 400 brother combinations have played MLB over the years.

CLOCKWISE: CAL RIPKEN, JR., BILLY RIPKEN, AND CAL RIPKEN, SR.

BASEBALL GLOSSARY

analytics: the study of numbers, patterns, and statistics

assist: a play, or part of a play, in which a fielder throws the ball to another fielder who makes a putout

at bats: times that a player faces a pitcher

bags: another word for bases

ball: a pitch that the umpire says did not cross the strike zone

Baseball Hall of Fame: a museum in Cooperstown, New York, that honors the best players, managers, and others in baseball history

base hit: a batted ball that results in the hitter reaching base

basepath: the straight line between each base

batting average: the ratio of hits per at bat

blown save: a situation in which a relief pitcher enters with his team ahead, but he gives up runs that tie the game or put his team behind

box score: a grid of text and numbers that records all the important information from a baseball game

centrifugal force: the physical pressure exerted outward from a spinning object

circumference: the distance around a circle

count: the number of balls and strikes on a batter

curveball: a pitch thrown so that it moves down and sideways

dinger: a nickname for a home run

error: a mistake by a fielder that results in a batter reaching base or advancing to another base

extra-base hit: a double, triple, or home run

fielding: the act of catching and throwing the baseball

fielding average: the ratio of errors to total chances

foul ball: a batted ball that lands outside the white foul lines on the field

general manager: a person who puts together the roster of a baseball team

Gold Glove: an award given each year to the top fielders at each position in each league

grand slam: a home run hit with the bases loaded

launch angle: the degree at which a ball leaves the bat when struck

Little League: an international organization of baseball and softball for young people

long ball: nickname for a home run

magic number: the number of combined wins for a first-place team and losses for a second-place team that will clinch a championship for the first-place team

no-hitter: a game in which one team's pitcher or pitchers do not allow the other team a hit

perfect game: a game in which the starting pitcher does not allow the other team even a single base runner

pitcher's mound: the raised dirt area at the center of the diamond

pitching rubber: the rubber slab at the center of the mound that a pitcher must start each pitch from

plate appearance: any time a batter steps up to hit

pop time: the period from when a catcher receives a baseball to when his throw reaches the infielder's glove

pro: short for professional, a person paid to play a sport

putouts: any fielding play that results in a batter or base runner being out

range: the area a fielder can cover

range factor: a stat that compares how much area a fielder covers

retired number: a uniform number that a team designates as never to be worn again in honor of a great player who previously wore the number

runs batted in: a stat that counts runs scored due to a batter's success

sabermetrics: the study of baseball statistics, usually new and complicated ones

sacrifice: to make an out with the purpose of helping your teammate advance on the bases

scout: a baseball expert who works for an MLB team and whose job it is to find talented high school and college players to recommend as future players for a team

screwball: a twisting pitch that usually curves down and toward a batter

slash line: a stat that shows the measurements of batting average, slugging average, and on-base percentage

slider: a twisting pitch that curves in a flatter plane than a curveball

southpaw: nickname for a left-handed pitcher

spherical: describing the shape of a ball

stats/statistics: numbers and information gathered to record happenings in sports

stolen base: the result of a base runner advancing from one base to another by running during a pitch and without the ball being hit

strike: a pitch that the umpire says passes through the strike zone or a pitch that is swung at and missed by the batter

strike zone: the area over the plate and between the chest and knees of the batter

swing path: the movement through space of a bat when it is swung

tater: nickname for a home run

toe the slab: nickname for pitching

total bases: a stat that records how many bases a batter earns through hits, with one base for a single, two for a double, and so on

velocity: speed

walk (base on balls): the result of a pitcher throwing four pitches outside of the strike zone to one batter

weight drop: a measurement for a baseball bat that compares the amount of weight to the length of the bat

wild pitch: a pitch that eludes the catcher and lets base runners run to the next base while the catcher runs after the ball

World Baseball Classic: a tournament that matches national baseball teams

World Series: the annual championship of Major League Baseball, played between the champions of the American and National Leagues

ABBREVIATIONS

AB	at bat		**MLB**	Major League Baseball
AL	American League		**NCAA**	National Collegiate Athletic Association
BA	batting average		**NL**	National League
BABIP	batting average on balls in play		**OBP**	on-base percentage
BB	base on balls (a walk)		**OPS**	on-base percentage plus slugging average
DRS	defensive runs saved		**PO**	putout
E	error		**RBI**	run batted in
ERA	earned run average		**SA**	slugging average
ERA+	adjusted earned run average		**SAC**	sacrifice
FIP	fielding independent pitching		**SB**	stolen base
H	hit		**SF**	sacrifice fly
HBP	hit by pitch		**TB**	total bases
HR	home run		**UZR**	ultimate zone rating
K	strikeout		**VORP**	value over replacement player
L	loss		**W**	win
LIPS	late inning pressure situations			
LL	Little League			
LLWS	Little League World Series			

CREDITS

Diagrams and illustrations, unless otherwise noted, by Fan Works Design

AS: Adobe Stock; GI: Getty Images; SS: Shutterstock

COVER: (bat), photastic/SS; (glove), Victor Moussa/AS; (pitcher), Al Tielemans /Sports Illustrated via GI; (baseball), Iasha/SS; (batter), moodboard/AS; (helmet), Science Photo Library RF/GI; (2nd baseman), Donald Miralle/GI; (catcher), Nicholas Piccillo/AS; (texture), Yevgenij_D/SS; spine (baseball), Iasha/SS; back cover (pitcher), Tom Wang/SS; (baseball diamond), Dots777/SS; (catching ball in glove), Bildagentur Zoonar GmbH/SS; **FRONT MATTER:** 1, Maks Narodenko/SS; 2, Icon Sportswire/GI; 3, Maks Narodenko/SS; 4-5, Rob Carr/GI; 6, Mary DeCicco/GI; 7, Greg Nelson/GI; **CHAPTER 1:** 8, AS; 10 (UP), Adam Vilimek/SS; 10 (CTR), Photo12/Universal Images Group/GI; 10 (LO), Marie C Fields/SS; 12 (LE), Arina P Habich/SS; 12 (RT), Irina Marwan/GI; 12-13, adamkaz/GI; 13, Bob Levey/GI; 14 (UP), Tim Boyle/GI; 14 (CTR), Peter Joneleit/CSM/SS; 14 (LO), Jeff Wilson/SS; 15 (UP), Tom Szczerbowski/GI; 15 (CTR), Maks Narodenko/SS; 15 (LO), Rich Schultz/GI; 16 (UP), Mike Zarrilli/GI; 16 (CTR), George Rinhart/GI; 16 (LO), Louis Requena/GI; 17 (UP), Billie Weiss/Boston Red Sox/GI; 17 (LO), Alex Trautwig/GI; 18 (UP), Everett/SS; 18 (CTR), Mark Rucker/Transcendental Graphics/GI; 18 (LO), Hollywood Photo Archive/Mediapunch/SS; 19 (UP), Bettmann/GI; 19 (LO LE), Focus On Sport/GI; 19 (LO RT), Ron Vesely/GI; 20 (RT), Maks Narodenko/SS; 20 (UP), Mtsaride/SS; 20 (LE), Jonathan Moore/GI; 20 (CTR), Lee Jin-Man/AP/SS; 21 (UP), Shane Bevel/GI; 21 (CTR), Icon Sportswire/GI; 21 (LO), Mark Dadswell/GI; 22 (UP), Anton Starikov/SS; 22 (CTR), Theerasak Tammachuen/SS; 22 (LO), East/SS; 23, JoeSAPhotos/SS; **CHAPTER 2:** 24, AS; 26, Stephen Brashear/GI; 27, 4×6/GI; 28 (UP), John Bazemore/AP/SS; 28 (LO), Bettmann/GI; 29, Elaine Thompson/AP/SS; 30, Otto Greule Jr/GI; 31, The Conlon Collection/GI; 32 (UP), Dilip Vishwanat/GI; 32 (LO), The Sporting News/GI; 32-33, Scott Cunningham/GI; 33 (UP), Photo File/GI; 33 (LO), David Lee/SS; 34 (UP), New York Daily News Archive/GI; 34 (LO), Carlo Allegri/GI; 35 (UP), Transcendental Graphics/GI; 35 (LO), Ron Vesely/GI; 36, Scott Taetsch/GI; 37, Michael Owens/GI; 38 (UP), Fort Worth Star-Telegram/GI; 38 (LO), Jason Miller/GI; 39, Richard Rodriguez/GI; 40 (UP RT), Bettmann/GI; 40 (UP), Maks Narodenko/SS; 40 (LO), Bettmann/GI; 40 (CTR LE), New York Times Co./GI; 40 (CTR RT), Focus On Sport/GI; 41 (UP), Joe Robbins/GI; 41 (CTR), Jason Szenes/EPA-EFE/SS; 41 (LO), Peter Joneleit/CSM/SS; 42, SDI Productions/GI; 43 (LE), Bogdan Sonjachnyj/SS; 43 (RT), Jacek Chabraszewski/SS; **CHAPTER 3:** 44, Sam Edwards/GI; 46 (LE & RT), Transcendental Graphics/GI; 47 (UP), Jonathan Moore/GI; 47 (LO), Nick Laham/GI; 48, Transcendental Graphics/GI; 49, Ron Vesely/GI; 50, Rob Carr/GI; 51 (UP), Pool/GI; 51 (LO), Peter Muhly/GI; 52 (UP), New York Daily News Archive/GI; 52 (LO), Kevork Djansezian/GI; 53, Lisa Blumenfeld/GI; 54 (UP), Spectruminfo/SS; 54 (LO), John McCoy/GI; 55, Darin Wallentine/GI; 56 (UP), Boston Globe/GI; 56 (LO), G Fiume/GI; 56 (CTR), Duane Burleson/AP/SS; 57 (UP), Dilip Vishwanat/GI; 57 (LO), Paul Bereswill/GI;58 (UP RT), Everett/SS; 58 (UP LE), Maks Narodenko/GI; 58 (LO LE), George Strock/GI; 58 (LO RT), Bettmann/GI; 59 (UP), Herb Scharfman/Sports Imagery/GI; 59 (LO), Al Bello/GI; 59 (CTR), Ezra Shaw/GI; 61, Thinkstock/GI; 60, subjug/GI; **CHAPTER 4:** 62, Dmytro Aksonov/GI; 64 (UP), Scott Taetsch/GI; 64 (LO), Jamie Squire/GI; 65, Tannen Maury/EPA-EFE/SS; 66 (UP), JoeSAPhotos/SS; 66 (CTR), Ronald C. Modra/GI; 66 (LO), Focus On Sport/GI; 67 (LE), Bob Levey/GI; 67 (RT), Dylan Buell/GI; 68 (UP), Christian Petersen/GI; 68 (CTR), VGstockstudio/SS; 68 (LO), Paul Bereswill/GI; 69, Icon Sportswire/GI; 70 (UP), sirtravelalot/SS; 70 (CTR & LO), Icon Sportswire/GI; 71, Diamond Images/GI; 72, Maks Narodenko/SS; 72-73, Greg Fiume/GI; 74 (UP), Diamond Images/GI; 74 (LO), Harry How/GI; 75 (UP), B. Bahr/GI; 75 (CTR), Photo File/GI; 75 (LO), Bruce Bennett/GI; 76 (UP), Mike Stobe/GI; 76 (CTR), Marc Serota/GI; 76 (LO), Ron Vesely/GI; 77 (UP), Thearon W. Henderson/GI; 77 (LO), Kansas City Star/GI; 78 (UP), Dan Kosmayer/SS; 78 (LO), Pixel_Pig/GI; 79, Kent Kobersteen /National Geographic Image Collection; **CHAPTER 5:** 80, sshepard/GI; 82, Peter Joneleit/CSM/SS; 83, Focus On Sport/GI; 85, Otto Greule Jr/GI; 86, Daniel Shirey/GI; 87 (UP), Patrick Semansky/AP/SS; 87 (LO), Lane Stewart/GI;88, Denis Poroy/GI; 89 (UP), Greg Nelson/GI; 89 (LO), Bob Levey/GI; 90 (UP), Joe Robbins/GI; 90 (LO), Rich Pilling/GI; 91, Robert Clay/Alamy Stock Photo; 92, Transcendental Graphics/GI; 93, ESPN.com;94 (LE), Marko Poplasen/SS; 94 (RT), FatCamera/GI; 95 (LO LE), Maks Narodenko/SS; 95 (LO CTR LE), HomeArt/SS; 95 (LO CTR), P_Art/SS; 95 (LO CTR RT), paulista/SS; 95 (LO RT), Supawat Punnanon/EyeEm/GI; **CHAPTER 6:** 96, Eugene Onischenko/SS; 98, Jay Gula/GI; 99, Jamie Squire/GI; 100 (UP), Bettmann/GI; 100 (CTR), Billie Weiss/Boston Red Sox/GI; 100 (LO), Bettmann/GI; 101, The Washington Post/GI; 102 (UP LE), Maks Narodenko/SS; 102 (UP RT), Louis Requena/GI; 102 (LO LE), Photo File/GI; 102 (LO RT), Focus On Sport/GI; 103 (UP RT), Justin K. Aller/GI; 103 (UP LE & LO LE), Bettmann/GI; 103 (LO RT), New York Daily News Archive/GI; 104 (UP), Preston Mack/GI; 104 (CTR), Nick Laham/GI; 104 (LO), Jim McIsaac/GI; 105, Bettmann/GI; 106 (UP), Kevork Djansezian/GI; 106 (LO), Omar Torres/GI; 107, Steve Grayson/GI; 108 (LE), Peter Aiken/GI; 108 (RT), Larry French/GI; 109 (UP), Owen C. Shaw/GI; 109 (LO), Rob Carr/GI; 110, matooker/GI; 111 (UP), Joe McBride/GI; 111 (CTR), Yamada Taro/GI; 111 (LO), Erik Isakson/GI; **CHAPTER 7:** 112, Alex Kravtsov/SS; 114 (UP), New York Daily News Archive/GI; 114 (LO), Warren Wimmer/GI; 115 (LE), Transcendental Graphics/GI; 115 (RT), Hy Peskin Archive/GI; 116 (UP), Maddie Meyer/GI; 116 (LO), Ezra Shaw/GI; 117, Photo File/GI; 118 (LO), Andy Cross/GI; 118 (UP), Bettmann/GI; 119 (LO), Bettmann/GI; 119 (UP), The Stanley Weston Archive/GI; 120 (UP), Diamond Images/GI; 120 (LO), Focus On Sport/GI; 121 (LE), Ronald C. Modra/GI; 121 (RT), Focus On Sport/GI; **END MATTER:** 122 (LE), Shoji Fujita/GI; 122 (RT), Bryan Eastham/SS; 123, Jamie Roach/SS; 124, Bruce Leighty Sports Images/Alamy Stock Photo; 128, Ddukang/GI

INDEX

Illustrations are indicated by **boldface.**

MATH TEACHER REFERENCE

ALGEBRA AND ARITHMETIC

- **Formulas:** pages 26, 30, 31, 50, 51, 69, 76, 84, 86, 89, 90
- **Percentages:** pages 51, 53, 89

GEOMETRY

- **Angles and arcs:** pages 36, 65
- **Shapes:** pages 11, 20

MEASUREMENT

- **Circumference:** pages 15, 20
- **Speed:** pages 56, 57, 64
- **Spin:** page 54
- **Straight line:** page 11, 20

STATISTICS

- **Averages:** pages 42, 50, 67
- **Batting average:** pages 28, 29
- **Graphical representation of data:** pages 29, 37, 67, 95

NATIONAL GEOGRAPHIC and Yellow Border Design are trademarks of the National Geographic Society, used under license.

The ESPN logo is a registered trademark of ESPN, Inc.

Since 1888, the National Geographic Society has funded more than 12,000 research, exploration, and preservation projects around the world. The Society receives funds from National Geographic Partners, LLC, funded in part by your purchase. A portion of the proceeds from this book supports this vital work. To learn more, visit natgeo.com/info.

For more information, visit nationalgeographic.com, call 1-877-873-6846, or write to the following address:

National Geographic Partners
1145 17th Street N.W.
Washington, DC 20036-4688 U.S.A.

For librarians and teachers: nationalgeographic.com/books/librarians-and-educators

More for kids from National Geographic: natgeokids.com

This book is for the Wheezers, especially Gordo, who helped create my childhood love for baseball and all its numbers, players, stories, and thrills. And it's for Carl Yastrzemski, my boyhood hero.

—JB Jr.

Library of Congress Cataloging-in-Publication Data

Names: Buckley, James, Jr., author.
Title: It's a numbers game : baseball / James Buckley, Jr.
Description: Washington, DC : National Geographic Kids, 2021. I Series: It's a numbers game I Includes index. I Audience: Ages 8-12 I Audience: Grades 4-6
Identifiers: LCCN 2020000411 I ISBN 9781426371561 (hardcover) I ISBN 9781426371578 (library binding)
Subjects: LCSH: Baseball--Statistics--Juvenile literature.
Classification: LCC GV867.5 .B83 2021 I DDC 796.357021--dc23
LC record available at https://lccn.loc.gov/2020000411

For rights or permissions inquiries, please contact National Geographic Books Subsidiary Rights: bookrights@natgeo.com

Designed by Julide Dengel and Fan Works Design

National Geographic supports K–12 educators with ELA Common Core Resources. Visit natgeoed.org/commoncore for more information.

National Geographic would like to thank the following book team: editors Angela Modany and Kathryn Williams; project editor Erica Jacobs Green; art directors Julide Dengel and Amanda Larsen; photo editors Lori Epstein, Sarah Mock, and Matt Propert; fact-checker Michelle Harris; and design assistant Anne LeongSon. A special thank-you to math expert Gail Burril and baseball expert Matt Reid for their careful review.

Printed in Hong Kong
20/PPHK/1